IS SCRIPTURE STILL HOLY?

IS SCRIPTURE STILL HOLY?

Coming of Age with the New Testament

A. E. Harvey

WILLIAM B. EERDMANS PUBLISHING COMPANY

GRAND RAPIDS, MICHIGAN / CAMBRIDGE, U.K.

Published 2012 by

Wm. B. Eerdmans Publishing Co.

2140 Oak Industrial Drive N.E., Grand Rapids, Michigan 49505 /

P.O. Box 163, Cambridge CB3 9PU U.K.

Printed in the United States of America

18 17 16 15 14 13 12   7 6 5 4 3 2 1

Library of Congress Cataloging-in-Publication Data

Harvey, A. E. (Anthony Ernest)

Is scripture still holy?: coming of age with the New Testament / A. E. Harvey.

p.   cm.

Includes bibliographical references and index.

ISBN 978-0-8028-6808-4 (pbk.: alk. paper)

1. Bible. N.T. — Criticism, interpretation, etc.   I. Title.

BS2361.3.H37   2012

225.1 — dc23

2012020291

www.eerdmans.com

Contents

v

Preface

⟨≋⟩

The origin of this book lies in a collection of sermons to which I was invited to contribute marking the fortieth anniversary of the publication of John Robinson's *Honest to God*. I found myself wondering whether, after a lifetime of study and teaching, I had yet become "honest" to the New Testament. Was my thinking in tune with modern developments in related disciplines and with social and religious circumstances which seem to call into question the very concept of "Holy Scripture"? Or was it still governed by unexamined assumptions inherited from the past?

This short book is a tentative and necessarily incomplete attempt to answer some of these questions. It contains some considerations which I believe should be taken more seriously by scholars than is usually the case, but for the sake of a wider readership I have done my best to avoid using technical language or assuming specialized knowledge; and I have not encumbered the text with notes and references. Informed readers will recognize the sources of my argument and where I have diverged into paths recommended by my own judgment; others will, I hope, be grateful not to be distracted by an elaborate apparatus of scholarly discussion and secondary sources.

The first chapter was delivered as the Lily Montague Lecture to the London Society of Jews and Christians in 2009. I am grateful to the Society for permission to use and adapt it for this purpose. Other parts of the book have been the subject of more informal lectures and discussions. I am grateful to all the participants, and particularly to those friends and former colleagues who have generously offered me correction, help, and encouragement and have saved me from many errors and infelicities. I am humbled by their acumen and deeply indebted to them for the careful attention they have given me.

A. E. H.

CHAPTER I

Coming of Age

⸺✺⸺

The title of this chapter is a deliberate allusion to Dietrich Bonhoeffer. Bonhoeffer was one of the first twentieth-century Christian theologians to take seriously the environment of a world which can do perfectly well without God: he argued (and his argument has particular authenticity, having been forged in conditions of captivity and threatened death in a Nazi prison) that if God is still to be believed in, then it must be as a God whose existence is no longer seen as necessary, or even perhaps desirable. Humankind has "come of age." It has emerged from the tutelage offered by traditional religious apologetics, and now stands open to persuasion only if God can be authentically proclaimed and witnessed to as a continuing presence in the world — and in Christian terms that means a presence so apparently powerless that it can be ignored and overridden as Jesus was, who came unto his own and his own received him not.

But, by modern standards at least, Bonhoeffer was surprisingly conservative in his approach to Scripture. Strongly influenced by Karl Barth, he used scriptural texts to support his arguments with little acknowledgment of the questions raised by critical scholarship and with barely any recognition that humankind might have "come of age," not just in its approach to God but in its response to the very notion of inspired and authoritative texts. He was writing, of course, some decades before the influx of adherents of other religions into Europe began to make the phrase "Holy Scripture" necessarily problematic. If people of equally profound faith rely on *other* "scriptures" in the same way that Jews and Christians rely on the Bible, the question has to be asked whether *any* scriptures can claim unique authority. Might not a world that has "come of age" with respect to God be one which has also "come of age" with respect to the whole notion of "Holy Scripture"?

This is more than an academic question. In public worship, for instance, Scripture has by no means such a secure place as in the past. In a typical funeral held in church, a Scripture reading may be supplemented, or even replaced, by texts which have caught the popular imagination as more credible and reassuring statements about life after death than anything in the Bible — Henry Scott Holland's "Death Is Nothing at All" has become one such favorite reading. As for the Old Testament, most congregations whose main service is a eucharist hear very little of it, and when they do they may well wonder whether the passage they have heard is more edifying than something that might be chosen from other literature.

Indeed, the word "holy" itself has been losing currency and now seldom appears in the same breath as "Bible" or "Scripture." Whereas earlier translations into modern languages were regularly called "The Holy Bible," and all Christian Scripture was known as "Holy Scripture," today many new versions appear without any such adjective. "The Revised English Bible," "The Jerusalem Bible," "The Good News Bible" — titles such as these are now regarded as perfectly acceptable, and to add the word "holy" may be thought almost quaint or archaic. "Bibles," like dictionaries or atlases, are simply books which are placed on a certain shelf in a library or a bookshop. Translations appear in contemporary, sometimes banal, language, and some editions have adopted the style of disposable paperbacks, sometimes with quite new titles, as if the fact that the title by which the book has been known and revered for centuries is now irrelevant. What matters, it seems, is to make the text accessible and attractive to any reader looking for something to read at a station newsstand (even if, once on the train, they may be disappointed to find it is only a Bible after all!). The Bible, we have been told, is "like any other book."

STC

But of course it is not as simple as that. There are indeed certain respects in which the Bible *is* like other books — it is published, it is printed,

2

it may be translated into other languages, it contains texts in literary genres which occur elsewhere. But equally it is *not* like any other book. It is certainly not like *modern* books, which first appear in many copies at once in a printed edition. It comes to us from the ancient world, and it was copied by hand for more than a millennium and subject to the accidents and textual corruptions which were liable to befall any ancient text before the invention of printing. Moreover, it is not so much a book as a collection of books, some of which have no literary parallel even in the ancient world; and the collection itself was made, not haphazardly or for literary reasons, but according to principles that were religious and have no exact parallel in any other religious literature. There is a sense, in other words, in which the Bible, far from being "like any other book," is profoundly different from all other books.

But that could be true of other works of literature — Homer, for instance, or Dante or Shakespeare. Does this difference justify us in treating the Bible differently from other writings which we call "classics"? For most of its history, it is true, it has received treatment which gave it a special place among books. Normally printed in double columns (unlike most books except dictionaries and telephone directories), bound in fine leather, and often set in a place of honor in the house, handled reverently, and attended to respectfully, it was certainly not regarded as just another book, and it seemed to command an allegiance that (at least in the West) was given to no other set of writings. Indeed, when the text began to be called into question for its historical reliability in the seventeenth century, or for its compatibility with the advance of scientific knowledge in the nineteenth, and still more when it was systematically subjected to the critical investigation of sources and literary relationships in the twentieth, there were many who felt that such interrogation of a revered book was inappropriate and even shocking.

But this resistance could not stop the advance of modern critical methods, and some demotion of the Scriptures from their former privileged place became inevitable. To take only one example: from the sixteenth century, when the New Testament began (in the West) to be studied seriously in the original Greek, until the mid-nineteenth century, it seemed as if the language in which it was written was a unique linguistic phenomenon. It

3

was strikingly different from classical Greek; and apart from that of the Greek Old Testament (the Septuagint, another "sacred" text) with which it had clear affinities, there was no known parallel to it in the ancient world. Just as biblical Hebrew could be regarded as holding a privileged place among human languages as the vehicle for the revelation of God's will for the people of Israel, so, it seemed, the revelation of the new covenant in Jesus Christ was conveyed in a language providentially created for the purpose — some went so far as to call it the "language of the Holy Ghost." But then came the discovery of hundreds of letters and administrative documents written on papyrus in the centuries immediately before and after the New Testament. These revealed the existence of a spoken language — the *koinē* — that was evidently the matrix of New Testament Greek. What had previously been regarded as a "sacred" language, providentially created for the conveyance of divine truth, turned out to be the exact opposite: a basically functional and colloquial form of Greek that was the *lingua franca* for administrative and private correspondence throughout the eastern part of the Roman empire.

A similar development can be seen in the respect accorded to the contents of the Bible as a whole. It is well known that the canon of both the Hebrew and the Christian Scriptures was by no means established from the start. In each case it evolved over a period of centuries, and variations within it have caused divisions among believers — there were parts of the Old Testament, for instance, which were received by some sectors of the Christian church but relegated by others to a less authoritative category known as "Apocrypha." Nevertheless, for the greater part of the history of both Christianity and Judaism the extent of what was regarded as "Scripture" seemed to be established beyond controversy. But things are different now. Students of the Hebrew Scriptures can hardly leave out of account texts, or versions of texts, found only in the Dead Sea Scrolls; students of the gospels are expected to show familiarity with texts such as the *Gospel of Thomas,* a Gnostic writing which may preserve early and authentic material about Jesus; they may even have to come to terms with an entirely hypothetical document known as "Q," which consists only of material culled from the three synoptic gospels but which, by virtue of its selection and arrangement, is alleged to present a somewhat different account of Jesus from that of the canonical gospels. For the scholarly community and their students (many of whom will enter the ordained ministry), this enlargement of the field of study to other texts, along with the introduction of a whole range of critical methods, has been generally welcome and is now virtually taken for granted. By contrast, the more conservative adherents of the two religions tend to insist on a very clear demarcation between "Scripture" and other literature, and some churchgoers will even confine their reading to the King James Version, believing it to have acquired a measure of authority, if not actual "holiness," by virtue of its continuous and virtually exclusive use in the English-speaking world over a period of some four centuries. Between these extremes stand the great majority of present-day worshipers, gradually coming to terms with the proposition (taken for granted by those of their ministers who have been trained in modern critical methods) that Moses is not the author of every word in the Torah or that Jesus is not likely to have spoken all the words attributed to him in John's gospel, but still ready to accord to any text in the Bible an authority over their thinking and conduct which is not possessed by any other literature. How is this authority to be accounted for, and is respect for it still justified?

Divine Inspiration

There is of course one respect in particular in which the scriptures of a religion may be claimed to be authoritative and "holy." Both the Hebrew Scriptures and the Qur'an contain texts which purport to be the words of the holy God himself, imparting an indelible holiness both to the language in which this divine communication took place (biblical Hebrew or classical Arabic) and to the book in which those texts are preserved. Moses is said to have received the Law directly from God; the prophets say with absolute confidence, "This is the word of the LORD"; Muhammad faithfully passes on words spoken to him by an angel on behalf of Allah. It is true that the Christian Scriptures — the New Testament — are much less explicit in this respect than the Torah or the Qur'an. They nowhere say, or even imply, "Thus says the LORD." In Christian understanding, the revelation consists in the person of Jesus Christ. The words of the New Testament do not have the sanctity of direct utterances of God since they are a human record of the revelation, not the revelation itself. Their subject matter — the incarnate Son of God — certainly implies a certain "holiness"; it imparts considerable authority to the text for those who have come to accept the claims made in it for and by Jesus. But it is not necessary to believe (though it has often been believed in the past) that the creation of this record required divine intervention. Indeed, the entire weight of modern New Testament scholarship is on the side of those who believe that the texts came into existence through the normal operations of human remembering, recording, editing, and transcribing, acquiring their special authority only from their subject matter and their privileged degree of access to it. They may be (as they sometimes claim to be themselves) "inspired" by the Holy Spirit; but they are not, in themselves, the record of any speech-act of God. Indeed, there is little theological justification for the response which members of the Church of England (and, in many cases, Roman Catholics) are now required to make to the reading of Scripture during the liturgy. Even when the text has to do with such things as the treacherous murder of Sisera or the grisly fate of the ungodly in the book of Revelation, they are supposed to swallow their revulsion and say, "This is the Word of the Lord."

But surely, it may be said, if we accept that a text is "inspired," it will follow that it must hold a privileged place among all texts, whether or not it makes any claim to be a direct verbal mediation of a message from God. And, indeed, the "inspiration" of Scripture is the heading under which the doctrine of scriptural authority is normally formulated. But it is a doctrine which has proved extremely difficult to define, not least because inspiration itself is a slippery word with a whole gamut of secular uses, ranging from a schoolboy being inspired to pick up his pen to put a new idea into his essay to Rainer Maria Rilke being inspired to write a substantial portion of his *Sonnets to Orpheus* in a matter of hours. Even if the sense of the word is narrowed so as to be used only of some input from a transcendent or supernatural source, problems abound: given that an allegedly inspired prophecy, for instance, is conditioned, if not actually evoked, by a particular crisis in human affairs, must we not say that the crisis itself is part of what was inspired? But then, given the complexities of historical causation, must we not extend the argument and say that the events and circumstances which led up to the crisis were also inspired — and so on in an infinite regression, the whole course of history coming to be regarded as inspired, leaving us no way of distinguishing the original prophecy as a particular vehicle of inspiration? These difficulties, and many others like them, have frustrated all attempts to define an agreed doctrine of inspiration, and we do not get much further by invoking it as a justification for calling any particular writing "holy." We may perhaps make a little more progress with the kindred concept of "revelation." The author of the last book of the New Testament had visions which took him as close to the presence of God as is possible for any human being, and when his account of this is called a "revelation," this word not only describes a particular kind of experience but also indicates that the source of it is a special and unrepeatable moment when the divine has impinged directly on the human. Indeed "revelation," along with "inspiration," is the term customarily used in theological discourse to describe the particular character and authority of writings which lay claim to recording some moment when God communicated with a human being. Scripture, we may say, is authoritative and holy because it delivers to us, in various forms and idioms, a revelation which God has graciously made of his nature, his intentions, and his demands.

That this is what in fact God has done is the basic presupposition of all three Abrahamic faiths. Indeed, it has been said that the unique contribution of Judaism to Western civilization, at least until that of older Asian religions became generally known, has been to have given credibility to the notion that intimations of the divine can be clothed in verbal form and transmitted in writing for the guidance and instruction of generations to come. And, indeed, it is arguable that such a transaction with a transcendent reality is not merely possible but philosophically plausible. Words, we now realize, are not merely mechanical agents of the speaker or the author; they are integral to the message, which would be impotent to convey meaning without them; they point to the existence of a reality beyond themselves to which they alone provide access. Moreover, in all our traditions, both exegetes and mystics have given testimony that a message may be found in the text which is deeper than its surface meaning and immediate context. Through meditation and prayer it can lead into an apprehension of profound realities. This testimony, it is true, has taken astonishingly diverse

7

forms down the centuries; nevertheless, it must count as evidence that these writings represent some form of communication — a message delivered by a messenger — and are not merely the literary creations of their human authors.

Such a conclusion, it may be, is made the more easily conceivable by the Christian doctrine of Incarnation. If God, as Christians believe, could be rendered present in human form, then the incarnation of this presence in words becomes a lesser mystery. As Pascal expressed it, "All words are an incarnation of thought. If we investigate the relation of their forms to the truths signified, we have the same mystery as the Incarnation." At the same time, this may pose a problem for Christians, in that they have to ask whether the God of the *Christian* religion could ever be conceived as having acted in this way. To return again to Bonhoeffer: the message of Jesus seems to be that God is (as it came to be expressed in a Christian writing of the second century) a God not of coercion but of persuasion; he does not force his will on us or compel us to believe. In Bonhoeffer's understanding, he is a weak presence who wins human hearts and minds only by loving persuasion, never by a display of power. Could such a God ever have broken his own rules to the extent of trumpeting his message to humankind in such a way that it could not be gainsaid? If he has given a definitive "revelation" of himself at a particular moment in time, so commanding obedience and molding human conceptions of himself, has he acted contrary to his own nature and to the freedom with which he has endowed humankind?

This question is particularly relevant to a further tactic, which was devised as recently as the nineteenth century to restore an element of allegedly damaged or neglected "holiness" by claiming that the text of Scripture is "inerrant." God cannot be in error, the maxim ran; therefore, he cannot lead us into error. According to this doctrine, the authors of Scripture had supernatural knowledge which enabled them to make accurate predictions of events in the distant future and to take account of factors which would be appreciated only by subsequent generations. In response to Darwin's theory of evolution, many authoritative churchmen (though not so many devout Jewish interpreters) labored to defend this concept of inerrancy either by seeking to disprove the theory of evolution or by showing that the account of creation in Genesis, even when read as literal history, was somehow compatible with modern scientific observation — an enterprise which, however implausible it may seem to outsiders, is still very much alive today among so-called "creationists." These people are assuming that the words of Scripture, regardless of the time and circumstances in which they were written, have a supernatural status which allows their readers to ignore or override factors which have become known only centuries later. For such an assumption there is no justification, either in Scripture itself or in theology. As Galileo's friend Cardinal Baronius put it (echoing St. Augustine), "The Holy Spirit did not intend to show us how the heavens work, but only how we may get there." As we shall see later on, a concept of "holiness" which implies literal inerrancy is one which is both theologically and philosophically indefensible and is rightly rejected by the majority voice of a generation which has, in this respect, genuinely "come of age."

What Sort of God?

And here, perhaps, we get to the heart of the matter. Part of what it means to say that human beings have "come of age" is that we are learning to come to terms, in our religion as well as our science, with the sheer immensity of time and space in which our existence is located. The universe is steadily expanding to unimaginable distances before our very eyes; the period during which the human species has evolved to its present form is reckoned in millions of years in which our recorded human history is but a momentary episode. Even within that brief episode the development of the human potential for exploration and control of our environment has grown exponentially. Can we seriously say that the God whom we believe to be the author of this immensity has confined himself to a particular moment in time and a particular human cultural environment in order to reveal something of himself that can be known by no other means? What of all the generations before this alleged revelation took place? What of all those races and cultures which by reasons only of geography or historical accident have had no access to this privileged communication of the divine? If God is on a scale compatible with creating such vast extents of time and space and allowing human beings such astonishing scope for adaptation to it, is not the very idea that he would pinpoint a single spatial and temporal coordinate for a crucial act of self-revelation one that now defies rational belief?

We may perhaps best approach this question by recalling a fundamental premise of most religions. It is by no means irrational or outmoded — indeed, it is common ground between the three Abrahamic faiths — to believe that a God exists who created the world; and we can go on to say, still quite rationally, that he did this, not by accident or out of caprice, certainly not as jest, but with serious purpose. We can further believe that he allowed to evolve in that world, again not as an accident or as an unforeseen consequence of natural development, human beings endowed both with free will and with a moral consciousness, capable of either cherishing their environment or ruthlessly exploiting it to their own ends.

From these fundamental beliefs about the relationship between God and the world it follows that, implied in the very act of creation, was the entrusting to human beings of all that part of the natural world that is accessible to them. In Qur'anic terms, humans bear the privilege and the liability of a divinely given caliphate; in biblical terms, we may say that theirs is a stewardship inherent in their dignity as beings created in the image of the Creator.

How would this caliphate, this stewardship, be discharged? Having created such stewards, what assurance was available to the Creator that the creation would be preserved and developed according to its ultimate purpose rather than be abused and exploited as a mere battleground of competing acquisitiveness and exploitation? Was any further factor introduced that would promote an outcome in accordance with the Creator's design? In theory, perhaps, no further intervention should have been necessary. Human beings were endowed with reason, and by this faculty they should have been well able to discern the benefits, as well as the obligations, of living in peace among themselves and in a harmonious relationship with the created order. But living beings guided only by rational and prudential principles would be like the imaginary horse creatures, the Houyhnhnms, described by Jonathan Swift in *Gulliver's Travels;* they would not be what we recognize as persons of genuinely free will, whose judgments may be clouded by passion and covetousness and whose moral worth consists in going beyond the dictates of prudence with acts of altruism, self-denial, and love. In the hands of human beings as we know them, with their potential both for destructive evil and for moral grandeur, how secure was the outcome which the Creator purposed? Was there not a risk involved right from the start, as even the Qur'an seems to recognize, telling us that the angels advised Allah against it (Surah 2.30)? Was there not even the possibility, as is hinted at in both Hebrew and Christian texts, that the Creator might himself be exposed to suffering at the consequences?

All such language is, of course, highly analogical. We apply such crudely human motives and characterizations to God at our peril, if they lead us to draw specific conclusions as to his nature and intentions. Purpose, risk, and suffering are not concepts which we can apply to God in any literal sense, even if our scriptures frequently encourage us to think in those terms. Yet we are dealing here with a claim that is accepted unquestioningly by the adherents of three major faiths — that is, by more than half the world's population — the claim that this same ineffable reality has nevertheless engaged with the world of human beings to the extent of communicating a verbal message which may be perceived as having a transcendent origin.

To investigate this claim, let us explore the concept of divine creation one stage further. We may, without irreverence or absurdity, suppose that it was within the design of the Creator to exercise some influence on his creatures even after setting them free in the world he had created, though still without infringing their freedom of decision by any form of physical coercion or overwhelming theophany. This is, after all, an intuition that lies deep in our religions. In Judaism it is expressed by the ancient maxim that a factor which existed at the very outset of creation was the name of the Messiah — a corrective influence, that is to say, was envisaged right from the start that would be inserted into world history at the appropriate time. In Christianity that same Messiah, now believed to have come in the person of Jesus, was grasped as the embodiment of a principle, a *logos,* that had existed from the very beginning. This intervention, in other words, whether in the past or in the future, must not be thought of as an afterthought of the Creator: it was in his mind from the outset, a necessary condition for the successful outcome of the creative enterprise.

If this was true of the definitive intervention represented by a messiah, then it can be conceived as true also of those lesser but still significant interventions that all three Abrahamic faiths bear witness to in their scriptures. To fulfill their stewardship, or discharge their caliphate, human beings would require some guidance. They would need, for instance, to be governed by law, much of which might indeed evolve from rational reflection upon the constraints on individual freedom required by social interaction. But if law was also to stimulate moral action, it would need to go beyond justiciable precepts; if it was to inspire truly neighborly and altruistic behavior, an input from resources other than those of reason was required, an input such as may credibly be thought to have been transmitted to us in the Torah or in the Qur'an. They would require also some distillation of wisdom acquired through human experience, which the literature of many cultures might provide, whether in the collected maxims of the Greek dramatist Menander or in the collections ascribed to King Solomon in the book of Proverbs. But, above all, they might be assisted by prophets — human beings divinely entrusted with a special message, intended not only for their immediate contemporaries but also for subsequent generations who would find in these oracles a challenge and an inspiration. In this way the unconditional claim of the Hebrew prophet, "Thus says the LORD," can be integrated into belief in a transcendent Creator God. Once we admit the possibility that the Creator left himself opportunity to give a touch on the reins of the wayward horses of the human soul, and so to exercise a persuasive but always non-coercive influence on his creatures, then it becomes reasonable to credit him with the resources for making the kind of communication with human beings which would trouble them and challenge them, without actually forcing them, to conform to his purpose and to their own true nature as stewards of his creation.

The Message and Its Medium

Yet even at the point of impact, any such divine initiative was inextricably mingled with human factors. The most immediate recipients of the message were persons whose individual characteristics and emotions were not suspended — they cannot be described in the same terms as the Pythian prophetess, who entered a trance and became the automatic mouthpiece of

Apollo's oracle (though some Jewish and Christian apologists of the early centuries tried to make use of this model). They delivered the message in their own style, in a language which was that of their neighbors and contemporaries, and which was subject to the ambiguities and variability of all human speech. To achieve more than temporary attention the message was then committed to writing, with all the attendant risks of scribal error and corruption in transmission. And at any time in the future (as has been systematically recognized only in recent decades) its meaning would depend on the presuppositions and expectations which each reader brought to it: "reader response" has to be recognized as a necessary variable in any transmission of information by means of the written word. At no point in the chain is the divine initiative separable from the human response or inured against the possibility of human error.

But the recognition of a necessary human element in the transmission of a divinely authorized message has further consequences which bear very directly on the question of authority and holiness. Scriptural texts have a long life. By virtue of their place at the very fountainhead of the apparently divine intervention which launches a religion, they are not replaceable, they do not become obsolete. Instead, they continue to be attended to and revered, centuries after they were composed, by readers whose language and culture have in the meantime undergone immense changes. They cannot therefore be understood, let alone applied to contemporary moral and religious issues, without the aid of skilled interpreters and exegetes. But here too is a point of entry for human fallibility. Indeed, it is not only that these interpreters and exegetes may make mistakes; they will find themselves faced with questions to which more than one answer may validly be given, and the guidance they give to the reader will reflect, not only the limitations of their technical skills, but the different schools and disciplines in which they have received their formation and the personal presuppositions which they bring to the text. All of this is very familiar to any student of the Talmud, much of which is a record of debates between different schools of interpreters.

But there is a further factor. If there is any one benefit which it may be claimed that Liberation Theology has brought to Christian theology, and perhaps also to Jewish reflection on the Bible, it is the now widely recognized influence which an interpreter's social background exerts on the understanding of a text. Just as almost the entire corpus of Christian spiritual writing from the early centuries until quite recently was the work of persons of leisure who assumed a similarly leisured form of life and freedom of action in their readers — thereby making their writings unusable by all but a small minority of Christians — so the interpretation of Scripture has been dominated by academics and religious who have had a relatively comfortable lifestyle and are a world apart from the realities of any working-class congregation in the poorer parts of the world. Jesus startled his followers by saying that it was harder for a rich man to enter the kingdom of heaven than for a camel to pass through the eye of a needle. Interpreters have fastened gratefully on the fact that he went on to say that with God all things are possible. The rich, we triumphantly pronounce (being relatively rich ourselves), will be saved after all through the unmerited grace of an omnipotent God — God has achieved the impossible by making wealth and poverty irrelevant to a person's salvation. It took a Liberation Theologian to call our bluff. Coming from a background where the poor are systematically exploited by the rich (and this was certainly Jesus' background also), he challenged us by suggesting that Jesus may actually have meant what he said. Of course, God may make exceptions, but otherwise for the rich to enter the Kingdom is virtually impossible! Without Liberation Theology we relatively well-off scholars might still have been maintaining that this saying of Jesus was about the miraculous grace of God extended to us all and was not the uncomfortable challenge to our lifestyle that Jesus is likely to have intended.

But not all styles and schools of interpretation are so benign. The history of the support that has been given by interpretations of the Bible to practices now generally seen as immoral, such as slavery, National Socialism, apartheid, discrimination against women or homosexuals, and even the use of the death penalty (as happened recently in the state of Texas), should be sufficient to demonstrate that no interpretation of Scripture can be self-authenticating. On the contrary, if it offends against any of the great moral principles that have been arduously fought for, often by religious people themselves — the dignity of the person, human rights, equality before the law, compassionate justice — it must be rejected as a misapplication, rather than an exposition, of the biblical message.

This means, of course, that no interpretation of Scripture can ever have the last word. The moment we admit, as we must, that human agency is involved at every stage of the transmission of the divine message, then it becomes impossible to appeal to Scripture for a final judgment. There is no such thing as its "literal truth." The meaning and significance of any speech act is subject to the correct comprehension of the language, an evaluation of the context, an ability to be aware of one's own presuppositions — in short, a host of factors all of which must be subject to human judgment and human error. To judge between one effort at comprehension and another there is no alternative to using criteria that derive from reason, from the treasury of human wisdom, and from the record of lives and actions that have been inspired by one interpretation rather than another and have manifested the moral and religious qualities acknowledged by all to be for the good of humanity. We may still justifiably claim that we can "live by the Bible," or show absolute obedience to the Qur'an, in the sense that our scripture is a source of guidance and instruction that is crucial in the formation of our view of the world and our personal lifestyle. But the quest to find in it specific rules of conduct, permanently valid articles of belief, or decisive formulations of religious practice must now be seen to be flawed from the start if it fails to recognize that it can be appealed to only in the light of criteria that have their origin outside itself.

Requirements for Holiness

What, then, are these criteria? I have already suggested some: it is impossible to believe that an interpretation or application of Scripture that runs counter to hard-won principles of human rights and equality or to deep moral instincts of altruism and compassion is one which can be maintained simply by appeal to the alleged inerrancy and finality of the text. But there is a further criterion which may have crucial importance, and which is a further inference which arises from the very concept of God. "No one has seen God at any time." No irrefutable evidence of his existence or his character is available. How then are we to know that he exists, that he is good, that he is powerful? There are, of course, what the Bible calls "signs" — apparent answers to prayer, significant weather phenomena, unaccountable military victories — but these tend to be ambivalent, and God seems to have an awkward reluctance to do what his justice seems to demand: the flourishing of the ungodly is a perennial challenge to belief.

So, we may ask, what resources remain to God to give assurance to human beings of his existence and his nature? And what if these too are exposed to the indifference or outright opposition which may be legitimate expressions of our sovereign free will? It is a question which haunts the scriptures of every faith. It attends the promulgation of a transcendent law through Moses, which seeks to compel compliance to the divine commands by the imposition of legal sanctions within the observant community; it is inherent in the very condition of prophethood, whether it be Jeremiah or Muhammad: the prophet suffers in his own person and destiny the pain of contempt and rejection; and it is a question which is never far from the mind of the author of John's gospel. As we shall see, the narrative of that gospel is structured around a long-drawn-out trial in which the question is repeatedly raised how an essentially noncoercive God can make himself known to an indifferent and unresponsive world. How does he respond to the human tendency not to accept either the message or the messenger?

If the divine Word "came unto his own, and his own received him not," what credibility can be given to the bearer of the message such that the reluctance of the hearers to believe may be overcome without the agent being empowered to bludgeon them into acceptance? To which the answer given is in the one word "witnesses." John the Baptist, certain followers of Jesus, and then, in subsequent generations, the lives, the conduct, the self-sacrifice, and often the manner of dying of those who accepted the message — these would stand as witnesses to its credibility and endorsements of its holiness. It is the same necessity of witness which lies behind the Qur'anic concept of *shahid*. For its impact on the world, the message of Allah as delivered to the Prophet relies on the words and deeds of those who faithfully live by it — and it is no accident that the Arabic word, like its Greek equivalent, soon came to mean both "witness" and "martyr." The indifference and rejection to which the self-revelation of a noncoercive God must be exposed is visited also on his witnesses, who may incur suffering and even death on his behalf. In the culture of the time, the character of the witness, rather than any other form of evidence, was the key factor in establishing the truth of a report; similarly, the authenticity of an allegedly divine revelation depended crucially on the manner of life, and often the acceptance of death, of those who sought to bear witness to it by communicating it to others. Today a similarly faithful witness continues to be a factor in the acceptance of any scripture as authoritative and holy.

Models of Authority

But there remains one question to ask: if our scriptures are holy only in the restricted sense that they claim a transcendent origin but are dependent on the vagaries of human transmission and reception for their application to the issues of modern life, how much authority can we ascribe to them? And how, in any case, do we now understand "authority"? The model most frequently appealed to is political: our governments have authority over us, defining our rights and obligations and determining the penalties we shall pay for transgressing the laws they make. Similarly, for a religious person, Scripture may be said to speak with the authority of the divine Governor of the universe, who has created human beings with certain rights and obligations and lays on them moral and religious demands, with penalties for those inevitable failures to conform which seem to be endemic in human nature. Unfortunately, the political model gives us very little help. The source of political authority has been the subject of intense philosophical debate down the centuries. At one time it was generally assumed to derive from God; subsequently it was looked for in human reason or in a supposed "contract" between governed and governors. Today it is looked for most eagerly in the principle of democracy: government is "authorized" by the fact of having won a majority of votes in an election. Yet this model is found woefully inadequate even for political theory. The evident shortcomings in the practice of all modern democracies force one to recognize that political authority must rest on a broader base than periodic elections. It depends (as we have become vividly aware in recent years) on such things as the known moral integrity of politicians, the degree of public consultation that has taken place, the extent to which the policies of the party in power protect the interests of all and not just a part of the electorate, and so forth. If these factors are neglected or transgressed, the authority of government is forfeited. Authority is by no means something which, once acquired, remains an unquestioned possession.

And this, perhaps, yields a clue toward a formulation of the kind of authority the Bible may now be said to possess and the claims which may be made for placing it in a different category from other books. That religious authority may be understood along the lines of political authority, and vice versa, is not a new concept: inscriptions survive from the time of the Emperor Hadrian, if not before, in which administrative edicts are entitled *hiera grammata,* holy writings. But political experience has taught us that authority is not a fixed attribute. Once acquired, it needs to be constantly justified and maintained. It must be repeatedly shown not to rest on false claims or fallacious arguments. Its credentials must be constantly reviewed, its exercise monitored, its place in the contemporary world of values seen to be defensible and appropriate. What this means, in the case of the Bible, is that, to the extent that it claims to convey historical information, it must be shown to have at least the credentials of other ancient historical writings; that as a foundation document for a religion it must have the necessary intelligibility and consistency; that for the nourishment of the liturgical and devotional life of the faithful it must have linguistic and imaginative depth; that to continue to be treated as an ethical guide its stance on moral questions must continue to be found relevant; and that when it is read and studied by those who accept its authority, it reliably relates them to their past and points them toward a credible and inspiring future. If a body of scripture is found to fail these tests, it must forfeit its authority. If it passes them, it may claim continuing authority subject to the vagaries of human transmission and application already mentioned.

The chapters that follow are an attempt to show that the New Testament does still pass these tests. The "coming of age" of which we spoke at the beginning has significantly raised the threshold which it must reach if it is to remain credible and authoritative; but it has also made it possible to take better account of the factors which limit the human ability to give an accurate report of past events and experiences and to receive that report as its author intended. Viewed in this light, the Christian Scriptures can be shown, I believe, still to command authority over adherents of the faith and to deserve respect from those outside it. And the grounds on which they may still be called "holy" are that, however imperfectly, they mediate to us some moment of experience in the past when the transcendent God in whom we believe intervened in the universe he had created in such a way as to influence his human creatures without ever coercing them or limiting their freedom of choice; and that the record of this intervention continues to beckon its readers and hearers toward a fuller understanding of the mystery of God and the nature of his expectations of us. Whether this continues to be the case depends on a host of factors which are continually changing; and Scripture must be constantly tested against newly emerging critical, literary, and moral criteria. But a factor which remains constant, and which for many may be decisive, is the continuing witness, often heroic, of those who have sought to make their lives an authentic response to these Scriptures while respecting those moral and religious principles which in recent centuries have helped humanity to pursue the project, which we believe to be that of the Creator, of a world governed by the arduously established values of justice, compassion, and peace.

CHAPTER 2

Checking the History

—∞∞∞—

The Acts of the Apostles

Does the New Testament give us "history"? The obvious place to test this would seem to be with Acts. The book is a consecutive account of a series of events in the life of the early church, told as a continuous narrative and following a scheme intended to show how the gospel, beginning in Jerusalem, reached the center of the known world — the city of Rome — and how Paul, the "apostle to the Gentiles," survived the attempts on his life and overcame all obstacles that were placed in his path in order to be able to preach and minister there himself (though the church had in fact already taken root in Rome before he got there). And more than this: Luke, the author, makes the point explicitly in a preface, both to Acts and to his gospel, that his work is based on serious research and is intended to provide its readers with the best available information on the subject. Surely this is exactly what we usually understand by "history."

But of course there are good historians and bad historians. Some get their facts right, some are careless; some are biased, most have some axe to grind. Our question is not so much whether Acts is "history" as whether this history is *reliable,* and for this purpose we must check it against as many known facts as we can; where we cannot we must get to know the author well enough to be able to decide if we can trust him. In the case of Acts (unlike the gospels) this is a possible enterprise. Whereas the story of Jesus un-folds in a small area of the Roman empire that was remote from the interest of Greek and Roman historians, and was such as to leave virtually no traces that would be likely to surface in official chronicles or material relics and in-scriptions, the narrative of Acts takes the reader into a number of Greco-Roman cities that are rich in archaeological data and involves persons who are otherwise known from the work of ancient historians or from inscrip-tions. At many points we can check its accuracy against other evidence, and form a judgment on the reliability of the author's sources and his compe-tence in using them. As we shall see, Luke passes this test (where we have the evidence to subject him to it) reasonably well. His references to persons known from other sources are generally correct, his chronology (but for one or two apparent howlers) is plausible, and his descriptions of places of-ten seem to betray firsthand, or at least good secondhand, knowledge. But this, unfortunately, is far from sufficient to establish whether we can regard him as a reliable historian. We need to look at the use he makes of his sources in more detail.

Acts falls fairly neatly into two parts. The first (chapters 1–12) is a narra-tive of the earliest years of the church, its foundation in Jerusalem and its first missionary movement across Palestine as far as Antioch in Syria. For this part there are very few points of contact with other historical records: the mention of the High Priests and their families in 4.6, the sudden death of Herod Agrippa in 12.23, and the chronologically confused reference to the rebellions of Theudas and Judas the Galilean in 6.36-37 are the only ones that can be checked against other chronicles of the time. But the second part (be-ing an account of the missionary journeys of the apostle Paul rather than the "acts of the apostles" in Palestine) takes the story into a more public domain and offers a number of cross-references with otherwise-known Roman offi-cials and with details of Roman administration. Where these can be checked, Luke appears to have done his homework quite carefully. Officials with names such as "politarchs" or "Asiarchs" seldom, if ever, occur in ancient lit-erature, but inscriptions prove that Luke has designated them correctly; he has faithfully reproduced the administrative arrangements in Philippi, rec-ognizing it to be a Roman colony (*kolōnia;* 16.12); and though for many years it was doubted whether there ever existed a named category of Gentiles sympathetic to things Jewish whom Luke consistently calls "God fearers," the publication in 1986 of an inscription from Aphrodisias in Asia Minor has now proved conclusively that "God fearers" was an accepted name for Gentile associates of the synagogue. In general, we can say that his knowledge of the physical and political environment was at least adequate for his purpose. The mistakes he makes (such, perhaps, as supposing that the official title of "shrine maker" in Ephesus meant that this person actually manufactured models of the famous temple there) are relatively trivial and need not affect our estimate of his reliability.

It is when we come to compare his account with the data that can be extracted from Paul's letters (or at least those which are unquestionably authentic — Romans, 1–2 Corinthians, Galatians, and Philippians), and still more when we place the speeches attributed to Paul in Acts alongside the beliefs and missionary strategies which Paul himself expounds in many parts of his own writings, that Luke's general credibility becomes much harder to maintain. Crucial to this comparison is the autobiographical section in Galatians 1–2, where Paul, with great emphasis on the accuracy of his own account ("God knows, I am not lying," 1.20), describes his first visits to Jerusalem after his conversion. The discrepancies between this and the relevant chapters of Acts (9–15) have perplexed scholars for generations and appear to be beyond reconciliation; and Paul's own account of his visits to Corinth and his difficulties there seems to bear little relation to the brief narrative in Acts 18.

Some of the discrepancies can doubtless be reconciled without too much difficulty. In part they can be explained as a difference of emphasis and perspective. Take the collection for the church in Jerusalem. This was evidently a matter of great importance to Paul: not only does he devote substantial paragraphs of his letters to encouraging the donors; he labors to dispel doubts about his own trustworthiness as an agent for the collection and to justify the lifestyle he deliberately adopted in order not to be a charge on the generosity of the churches which hosted him. Why does Luke barely mention this at all? It could be said that any accurate historical record would be bound to record a project which preoccupied Paul and his churches to this extent, particularly if (as the "we-passages" imply) Luke was a companion of Paul on several of his journeys. Yet a number of defenses are possible. Luke may simply not have known about it (unlikely, some will say, if he really shared sea voyages with Paul, with all the opportunity for talk and discussion they would have provided). He may have thought the matter of insufficient significance in the framework of his narrative to be worth mentioning (which is plausible). And, in any case, there are hints in the narrative that Luke was perfectly aware of it, or at least that his account allows for it. Why else, for example, was "a plot made against Paul by the Jews" in Corinth (Acts 20.3), except to embarrass him by robbing him of the money as he conveyed it to Jerusalem? Why did he make the long journey to Jerusalem by land, with a number of stops and detours, rather than taking a direct passage by ship, if not to foil attempts to steal the money, which would have been so much easier on a sea voyage? What, apart from the collection, could Luke have understood Paul to be referring to when he records him as saying, "I came to bring alms to my nation" (24.17)?

Other instances are similar: it does not take a great deal of ingenuity to find solutions to most of the apparent contradictions between Luke's account and Paul's own statements. As for the alleged difference between the "theology" of the speeches attributed to Paul in Acts and the dominant themes of Paul's Christian faith as displayed in his letters, this can again be explained as a matter of emphasis and presentation. It is certainly true that the major Pauline doctrines of justification by faith alone and the absolute equality of Jew and Gentile in the eyes of God are notably absent from Paul's discourses in Acts; but it is only reasonable to answer that for the most part this can be explained by the context. In Acts, Paul is represented as preaching to the unconverted and defending the faith against opposition; in the letters, he is addressing people who are already Christians (even if they sometimes share the prejudices and scruples of nonbelievers). Hence it should not be too surprising to find a clear difference of emphasis and tone and a different range of theological topics.

Many will justifiably be unconvinced by these arguments. But behind them lies an assumption which itself is open to question. Paul is writing about matters of which he has direct experience. His evidence is firsthand, and at times he even goes so far as to swear an oath that it is true. Surely, therefore, his account must be given priority over that of Luke, who, even if he was at times Paul's companion (which is itself open to question, as we shall see), had mainly to rely on second- or thirdhand reports or else on his own presumably less vivid memory. But is this the case? Modern biographers will always be glad to make use of the autobiography of their subject if it exists; but they will seldom regard it as an infallible guide to the course of a person's life. Memory distorts and confuses; past emotions color recollections; personal sensitivities prevent some things from being mentioned; imagination sometimes takes over where memory fails. In Paul's case we have particular reason to suspect that what he tells of himself (and this is remarkably little, considering how personal his letters often are) may be colored by the need to support an argument or mount a defense. May not his memory, like that of the authors of so many memoirs, have sometimes become confused with the passage of time and the press of conflicting emotions? And more than this: Paul was governed, more than most modern writers, by conventions derived from the theory and practice of rhetoric. When we read in 2 Corinthians a long list of the tribulations he endured, we may feel that we have struck a rich vein of information about his experiences. Flogged, imprisoned, shipwrecked — here is personal testimony indeed from which to build up a picture of the man and of the obstacles he surmounted in fulfillment of his mission. But then we find that it was a common device of Stoic philosophers to recite a list of their afflictions as a way of demonstrating the power of philosophy to strengthen their resolve and their endurance. These lists tend to have a common pattern: did Paul occasionally add one or two items just to add philosophical color to his account? Must we fault Acts for not mentioning some of them when they may not have happened at all?

Ancient Historiography

Much depends, of course, on the standards of accuracy and reliability which we bring to bear on the text. It is often said that ancient historians had very different ideas on these matters from ourselves, and that we must not expect them to show the same kind of respect for factual reporting and evidential support for their judgments as would be taken for granted today. But this is, at most, only partly true. Historians and philosophers in the ancient world thought a great deal about what is involved in writing history, and it would be quite wrong to suggest that they were cavalier with the facts. On the contrary, Luke in his prefaces is by no means the only one to stress the importance of *accuracy* in the historian's work. He uses a word — *akribōs* — which translators and expositors tend to overlook: it means "with accuracy, with precision," and goes along with the duty acknowledged by historians (even if they could not or did not always fulfill it) of securing good witnesses to the events they recount (if they were not there themselves) and even traveling to the places they describe; hearsay is rightly regarded as suspect. And we must add to this that they had far less available to them in the way of archives, reference books, and chronological tables than we are accustomed to, and had to rely a great deal more on personal and communal memory. It is true that they laid greater stress than we would find acceptable on making their narrative easy to read and a source of good entertainment; and this could involve selection and rearrangement of facts and episodes to an extent we should hardly regard as acceptable. Sometimes, of course, this may be due to the lack of some of the editorial devices by which modern historians can help the reader keep parallel events clear in their minds. A good example is the section of Acts (chapters 11–12) which describes events proceeding simultaneously in Antioch and Jerusalem. A modern historian might say, "We must now go back a few years to see what was happening in the other city"; but Luke simply says, "About that time. . . ." Neither he nor his readers will have been disturbed by the fact that what he is about to narrate in fact happened a few years earlier than the events he has just recounted. Nevertheless, we should recognize that ancient historians kept an eye on the pleasure which readers might derive from their narrative to an extent which would probably go against the conscience of most serious historians today.

Yet even when all this is allowed for, it is probably true to say that there is more in common between ancient and modern historians than there is to divide them. Both have an overriding concern to report the truth so far as they can obtain it; both seek to make a consecutive and understandable narrative out of the mass of data they have to handle; and both normally have a purpose in writing which goes beyond the mere recording of facts. Archives and hard evidence are not "history": the historian must select and interpret before the reader can draw instruction and pleasure from a recital of the past; and this selection will be guided by assumptions and predilections which derive from the cultural heritage in which the historian stands. These factors bear as much on the modern historian as they did on historians of antiquity. The professed ambition of Lord Acton and subsequent editors of the *Cambridge Modern History,* which appeared in 1902, was to use the modern resources and methods of historiography in order to create a definitive account of the past. This ambition was inherited from the heady days of the Renaissance, in which it was genuinely hoped and expected that all historical writing could be tested against the material records being discovered in profusion by archivists, antiquarians, and archaeologists. The spectacular advances in these spheres of study during the nineteenth century encouraged historians to think that they were within reach of the elusive goal of historical certainty and completeness. Had those responsible for the *Cambridge Modern History* succeeded in this ambition, no further edition would presumably have been needed: their work would have been truly (as they hoped) "universal." But it was soon realized that even monumental inscriptions carved in stone raise as many questions as they solve, and that the subjective judgment of the historian cannot be eliminated; indeed, it is an essential factor in the writing of history altogether. The dictum of Sir George Clark, the editor of the *New Cambridge Modern History* (1957), is nearer the mark: history, he remarks in his introduction to the first volume, is "a coherent body of judgments true to the facts" — and it is a body of judgments that must necessarily evolve in the light of every new discovery and every change of cultural presuppositions. When the author of Acts is assessed in this perspective, there is no reason to deny him a place among the serious historians of any age.

Sources and Methods

But what, in any case, were the resources which this author had at hand when he undertook to write "accurately" about the early days of the church and the missionary projects of the apostle Paul? Some insight into his methods may be gained (it is often suggested) by studying Luke's gospel. Assuming (as is usually done) that Luke had access to Mark's gospel when he composed his own, we can study the changes, the adaptations, and the omissions which he made, and discern from this some guiding principles of selection and editing which he presumably carried over into the second part of his work. But this observation is of limited application. We can assume that the material concerning Jesus, by the time Luke came to write his gospel, had acquired a certain solidity: Jesus' teaching and activities had been memorized, respectfully preserved, and carefully organized to form a consecutive narrative; the evangelist's freedom to elaborate on his sources was relatively limited. But none of this need have been the case when he came to write Acts. No such records are likely to have existed of the words and deeds of the apostles, and if they did they would not have been transmitted with the same reverence as those of Jesus; and still less would this have been the case for the other protagonists in a narrative which, so far as we know, was breaking new ground for a historian when it was written.

More significant, perhaps, is the question how far he drew on his own memories and experiences. It is generally assumed that Acts was written no earlier than the last decades of the first century (unless its failure to report the death of Paul, which took place around 64 C.E., indicates, as some maintain, that it was written before this had taken place). In that case at least half a century had elapsed between the events and the composition of the narrative. How much memory of these events would the author have had? The tradition that he was a companion of Paul is securely based on references to him in Paul's letters, where he is "beloved" or "a fellow-worker" (Col. 4.14; Phlm. 24; also 2 Tim. 4.10-11). This does not mean, of course, that he would have been well informed of all Paul's travels and missionary work. The crucial evidence here is the appearance of "we" in a number of the travel episodes in Acts. For no apparent reason, other (it might be supposed) than that at this point Luke actually joined Paul's party, the narrative suddenly drops into the first person plural. This would appear to give the authenticity of firsthand knowledge to the account; yet serious doubts immediately arise. Why does this "we" occur so suddenly in Acts 16.10 and disappear again without explanation just two paragraphs later? Why does it make only three appearances, equally unexplained, in the subsequent narrative? It is possible, of course, that, for reasons he tells us nothing about,

Luke was actually present with Paul only on the four occasions he actually mentions (though there would have been logistical problems involved in joining and leaving Paul's party at precisely those moments); but it is also possible that he used a travel diary (his own or someone else's) and almost unconsciously slipped into the first person when he was quoting from it. And there is a further possibility. Adopting the first person, either singular or plural, was a convention often used by ancient historians. Just as, if the historian was actually present and taking part in some episode he is recounting, he may use, not the first, but the third person (both Thucydides and Josephus speak of themselves as "he," not "I," when they appear in the narrative), so, when narrating the events on a journey (particularly a sea voyage), the narrator quite frequently dropped into the first person (either "I" or "we"), partly to give a flavor of firsthand authenticity to the account, partly to emphasize that the vicissitudes of sea voyages were such that they involved everyone on board, not just the protagonists of the story. In the light of this, it is surely no accident that the four we-sections in Acts all relate to journeys by sea, of which the most dramatic (the shipwreck in chapter 27) shows many affinities with other such accounts in ancient literature; and these regularly use the first person plural. Whether or not this is the true explanation of the we-passages in Acts, uncertainties must remain which make it impossible to claim with assurance that the second half of Acts is based on firsthand knowledge.

The Speeches in Acts

This reference to a literary convention points us in the direction of another factor. I have already observed that ancient historians were by no means as cavalier with the facts as is sometimes suggested. It is true that a work of history was expected to be both entertaining and morally instructive; but this did not mean that the historian was released from the obligation to report, so far as was possible, the true course of events. On the other hand the Greeks had never thought of history simply as a succession of events: the actions of human beings are directed by their thinking, and their thinking is expressed in words. Without an account of the words of military and political leaders — those words, at least, which were uttered on public occasions in the form of speeches — events were not held to be fully accounted for. History was always essentially "what was said and done," and the historian's task was necessarily to give an account of words as well as deeds.

It is well known that Thucydides was the first Greek historian to offer an explicit formulation of this principle, which is then exemplified throughout his *History of the Peloponnesian War* by the remarkable series of speeches he attributed to the leading protagonists. Unfortunately, the words in which he expressed this principle are somewhat ambiguous (*Histories* 1.22.1). On the one hand he admits to having freely composed the speeches according to his understanding of what it was necessary and appropriate for the speaker to say on each occasion; but on the other hand he refers not just to the "general intention" of the speaker but to "what was truly said" as constraints on what the historian could put into the speaker's mouth. This seems to imply that in some cases at least he had access to a record of what had been said, and that he felt obliged to abide by it, at least in general terms. But in many cases it is clear that he also felt not merely free but obliged to compose what he thought "fitting" if no such record existed. Precisely how he understood the procedure he recommended, how far he followed it consistently, and what sources, if any, he will have had that recorded the actual words or "intentions" of each speaker, have long been a matter of scholarly debate. What is certain is that subsequent historians were for the most part far less scrupulous than Thucydides in their efforts to reproduce what was "actually said," and their compositions often reflect the natural Greek instinct to have every issue debated with all the resources of rhetorical advocacy on either side. Inserting speeches into the narrative containing "what was demanded by each occasion" (Thucydides' phrase) was frequently extended to mean the exercise of attributing to the leading players the arguments for and against that the historian himself felt would have been relevant. Not all historians allowed themselves such liberties: the massive chronicle of the early Roman empire written by Polybius in the second century B.C.E. arguably represents a reaction in favor of more accurate speech-reporting. But the climate in which a historian of Luke's time undertook to write serious history was one which took for granted considerable freedom in the composition of speeches.

In comparison with his contemporaries, Luke is notably restrained in his use of speeches in Acts. They are short, concise, and to the point, and there is only one occasion (the speeches of Tertullus and Paul in Acts 24) on which two sides of the question are set out in opposing speeches in a manner that would have satisfied the Greek appetite for adversarial rhetoric. Nevertheless, the sermons and speeches fulfill an important function in the narrative. They justify the proclamation of the gospel as a legitimate development of the Jewish faith, and they explain the motivation of the apostles as they undertake their missionary work and confront the social and religious problems raised by their profession. Should we, then, look for evidence of historical sources lying behind these speeches, or should we assume that Luke was following the more liberal interpretation of the Thucydidean principle and freely composing what he thought "appropriate"?

Once again, there are grounds for taking either view. That Luke was being faithful to some record or actual recollection of what was said may be suggested at least by the speeches of Peter in the early chapters. The structure of these sermons, it has been argued, reflects the pattern of early Christian preaching which can be detected also in certain summaries that occur in Paul's letters; there are Semitic turns of phrase that suggest an Aramaic original; and there are apparent inconsistencies in certain theological expressions which Luke is hardly likely to have let pass if he was composing from scratch. These points, of course, are double-edged. It can be answered that the alleged pattern of preaching he reproduces is so basic to any proclamation of the Christian gospel that he would have been likely to follow it whether or not he had any record in front of him; that he was quite capable of deliberately adopting a style colored by apparently Semitic turns of phrase; and that it is no easier to account for his allowing theological inconsistencies to pass as an editor of already existing speeches than as the composer of new ones. Nevertheless, there is a certain probability to take account of. As we have observed, the gospel which preceded this "history of the church" contains reports of a great many "words," mainly those of Jesus; and these will have been remembered and transmitted with a high degree of care and reverence: Luke was certainly not free to write speeches for Jesus with the freedom of an ancient historian. But the moment we turn the page to the beginning of Acts and find that the main speaker is no longer Jesus but an apostle such as Peter, the situation changes dramatically. A speech was needed in this place, and even if a record existed, we need not think that it would have enjoyed the same scrupulous respect as the words of Jesus. Nevertheless, Luke had been working in his gospel within the discipline of an evangelist, obliged to reproduce Jesus' words with considerable fidelity. If he had some reliable account before him of the apostles' early discourses, would he not have shown something of the same fidelity in reproducing them? Should we not give him the benefit of the doubt even when the evidence is ambiguous?

Firsthand Evidence?

However this may be, the question presents itself differently in the second half of Acts, where the protagonist is Paul. Here we have on the one hand the possibility that Luke, as a co-worker with Paul, was physically present on some of the occasions when he reports a speech by Paul and could be working from his own notes, or (if he was not present) on the notes of others. This might seem a fitting explanation of the fairly dense argument in Paul's first recorded speech in Acts 13, where Paul is addressing his fellow Jews in the synagogue, is using quite technical methods for offering an "exhortation" from Scripture, and even appears, for once, to be alluding to one of his crucial doctrines, justification by faith (13.39). But on the very next occasion that a speech is reported (chapter 14), both the circumstances and the style are very different. The people of Lystra, amazed by a miracle that Paul has performed, attempt to offer him worship as if to a pagan god. To prevent them from committing such a blasphemy, Paul cries out, "We are human beings just like you!" But he then goes on with a short speech which strikes the modern reader as singularly irrelevant to the situation. It is a sermon (or, rather, a highly condensed summary of a sermon) such as any Jew might have given when addressing an audience of Gentile inquirers: there is a single God who has created all things and has left "clues" to his nature by ensuring a favorable natural environment for human beings. It is the same argument that is developed at much greater length in Paul's speech to the Athenians on the Areopagus (chapter 17), and this too is modeled on standard Jewish apologetic designed to convince Gentiles of the reasonableness of the Jewish faith, with just a twist at the end to bring the argument around to a Christian conclusion. Both speeches, in other words, seem to reflect the way in which it would have been natural for someone of Paul's Jewish background to address a pagan audience. That at Lystra, being the first point in the narrative when Paul is addressing non-Jews, gives a brief foretaste of the more highly developed argument which Paul later presented to the Athenians. Again, Luke may have been present himself on at least one occasion when Paul had to address such an audience, and made notes of the style he adopted; but equally he may have drawn on his own Jewish-Christian understanding of the way the gospel would need to be presented to Gentiles and have attributed to Paul some typical essays in the genre. Either way, we need not think he was misrepresenting Paul; but we certainly cannot be sure that he was reproducing anything Paul actually said on any particular occasion.

The same ambiguity belongs even to the account of administrative and legal proceedings against Paul in the last chapters of Acts. Here we have what purports to be an official letter from the military commander in Jerusalem to the Roman governor in Caesarea and two formal speeches, one by a professional advocate, in a formal hearing before the governor. In a modern text it would be assumed that when a document from the correspondence of an official was quoted, the author must have had access to it and be copying it accurately. But again, this assumption does not necessarily hold for ancient historians. There are several such documents both in Ezra and in Maccabees, but there are good reasons for believing that some, if not all, of them are artificial compositions; and Luke stood in the same tradition. It is highly unlikely that he had access to the governor's official files in Caesarea, but he was well able to compose the kind of letter which the military officer would have written, and he would certainly not have been thought to have departed from strict historical accuracy if he did so out of his own imagination. As for the forensic speeches of Tertullus and Paul, recent papyrus finds have demonstrated that many similar summaries of legal proceedings were preserved among official records, and Luke certainly had well-known models to work on. It seems improbable that he would have had access to an actual document in Paul's case; but there is no reason why, as a serious historian, he should not have composed authentic-looking summaries of the speeches he believed would have been made on this occasion; and it is through these speeches that the historian's purpose is fulfilled of enabling the reader to understand the motivation lying behind the actions of the parties to the conflict, the "words" behind the "deeds."

How, then, may we assess Luke's reliability as a historian? If we abandon the notion of history as an objective account of "the facts" available as a check on the interpretation placed on them by an individual historian, and acknowledge that any intelligible narrative of past events will involve a degree of selection, arrangement, and elaboration by the historian, then we must recognize that Luke was at the very least a reputable practitioner of the historian's craft according to the literary standards of his time, and that we are at least as well able to extract reliable information from his work as from that of others whose reputation is securely established. Of course, we must recognize that he told his story in such a way as to make it yield a message that was important to its Christian readers: the message that through the "acts" (but also the words) of the apostles, and particularly of Paul, the promise of Jesus had been fulfilled that the gospel would be preached in all the known world. In the interest of this message it appears that he smoothed over some rough places in the story, giving no indication, for instance, of the internecine struggles over matters of faith and practice within the young churches which form the vivid background to Paul's letters. He seems also to have used the normal device of set speeches to suggest that it was the driving force of a mission, first to the Jews, and then to the Gentiles, that inspired the apostles to endure the sufferings that were soon visited on all followers of "the Way." But none of this detracts from his basic reliability as a chronicler of the crucial events of this period: we simply have to learn (as with any historian) to make allowances for the particular interests and inclinations of the author, and form our own "coherent body of judgments."

The Gospels

When we turn to the question of the reliability of the gospels, we may do well to stay with Luke for a while, since we have gotten to know him as a writer accustomed to working within the discipline and conventions of a historian of his time. However different the material on which he was working in his gospel may have been from that of Acts, we may reasonably expect him to have had the same historical instincts and the same concern for truth. Indeed, of the two prefaces he affixed to the separate parts of his work, it is the preface to the gospel, not to Acts, which makes the explicit claim to be presenting the facts "accurately *(akribōs)* and in order." But in this case what were the "facts"? One of the few enduring inferences drawn by the form critics from the nature of the synoptic material has been that by studying the units out of which the gospels are composed rather than the consecutive narratives as a whole, it is possible to prove that sayings and episodes concerning Jesus existed independently of the context in which they now appear. From this it follows that beyond certain obviously fixed points in the story (such as the call of the disciples at the beginning, and the trial and crucifixion at the end) the evangelists will have had little means of placing the individual units of the material they inherited in a secure narrative sequence. The order in which most of the events took place or the sayings were spoken was certainly not one of the "facts" available to Luke; he simply appears to have accepted (as Matthew did, but John apparently did not) the basic sequence presented in Mark's gospel. Where he had more material to add, he evidently felt free to invent the contexts for it (as, for instance, in his extended narrative of Jesus' journey from Galilee to Jerusalem, which is clearly an artificial composition).

Critical Assumptions

But what of the material itself? The only clue we possess to the process by which an evangelist assembled the material for his gospel is given by the extraordinarily complex and intimate relationship the three first gospels have with each other. Given that there are substantial passages in which one evangelist uses virtually the same words and phrases as another, we make the assumption that there is only one way to explain this relationship: one gospel writer must have had the work of another before him. There is no hint in the synoptic gospels themselves to tell us which came first; but the most fruitful theory has been found to be that Mark was the first, and was used by Matthew and Luke. But if so, then both these later writers used Mark with a certain freedom. As we have remarked, they preserved the outline of the order, but they made omissions and additions to such an extent that each of their gospels has a distinct character. It is now generally accepted that these variations are to be explained by the particular interests and concerns of the evangelists, each of whom was seeking to present the story in such a way that it would answer certain questions and convey a message relevant to the situation of their hearers and readers. But this does not necessarily mean that we cannot trust them to be giving us true information. A series of tests has been devised to distinguish material purporting to go back to Jesus that is likely to be authentic and not the creation of the evangelists or their sources — that the portion of text in question is reported in several different places (such as the feeding of the several thousand), that it would have been embarrassing and therefore unlikely to have been invented by the early Christians (for example, the inscription on the cross), that it is unparalleled in the culture and therefore hardly to be attributed to anyone but Jesus ("Love your enemies," for example). Judging by these criteria, a substantial amount of what the gospels tell us about Jesus appears to be authentic.

And yet these criteria have been frequently challenged and modified. That of uniqueness is particularly vulnerable: what appears to be unparalleled today may turn up in some newly studied document tomorrow; and multiple attestation and embarrassment are both slippery analytic tools. Indeed, there is no way of decisively refuting anyone who holds that the Jesus material in the gospels, far from deriving from Jesus himself, was in fact the creation of the early church. Moreover this whole approach rests on assumptions which are far from secure. In 1976 J. A. T. Robinson threw down a challenge to the scholarly community with his book *Redating the New Testament,* in which he argued that the gospels were written a whole generation earlier than was then assumed by the great majority of interpreters —

that is, between 50 and 65 C.E. His arguments (elaborated in his posthumous book, *The Priority of John* [1985]) have not been generally accepted, and the reigning hypothesis is still that the gospels date from the second half of the first century; but Robinson's merit is to have exposed the fragility of the reasoning on which the accepted dating rests — namely, that the predictions of the fall of Jerusalem ascribed to Jesus in Mark 13, when compared with those in Luke and Matthew, suggest that Mark was written before, and Matthew and Luke written after, the actual event in 70 C.E., and that at least a decade would have been needed for Mark to have reached and been digested by the other evangelists, taking the dates of the completion of their gospels toward the end of the first century. It is not difficult to show that each link in this chain of reasoning is singularly weak. The so-called "apocalyptic discourse" in Mark 13 cannot be certainly dated before 70 C.E., nor the corresponding passages in Matthew and Luke to a later period: all three of them show a greater debt to scriptural prophecies of the ultimate destruction of Jerusalem than to any recollection of the events of 70; and we simply have no idea how long we must allow for one gospel to have reached another evangelist and then to have been adapted by him. Moreover, we must never forget that we know nothing about the way in which the gospels came into existence. The assumption that they have a literary relationship with each other — that is, that the similarities are to be explained by the writers having had access to each others' work — though it has held the field for at least two centuries and has proved immensely fruitful in many ways, is nevertheless no more than a hypothesis inferred from the practice of modern writers. Recently a rival theory has been proposed: that the differences are to be explained by the variations which are inevitably introduced when a story is repeated many times in a community setting: each evangelist should then be imagined more as a reciter of the Jesus story, prompted and monitored by the community which hears it, than as a writer composing his account in his study. Whether this new paradigm will replace the other remains to be seen. But once again it has reminded us of the fragility of the reasoning which underlies the usually accepted account of the gospels' genesis.

Yet even if the literary and historical criteria for authenticity remain problematical, and there is no assured way of deciding that any particular part of it gives us true information about Jesus, it is not necessary to resort to total skepticism. The view quite widely held by scholars in the mid-twentieth century, that the bulk of the Jesus material dates from long after his death, has not prevailed. The overall plausibility of the story, which has resisted countless attempts to dismiss it as far-fetched and improbable, and the respect shown to it by each of the evangelists, none of whom seems to have felt free to manipulate it to the extent we see happening, for example, in the "apocryphal" gospels, suggest that it would be unreasonable to suspect the gospel writers of being less serious about their commitment to tell an essentially true story than other ancient historians whose works we still use to establish a reliable account of events and personalities in the ancient world. Historical revisionism is something we are familiar with in modern history. It can seldom be decisively refuted; but if it is not supported by overall probability, it is generally superseded by a reversion to the traditional view, tempered by the more searching analysis of the material which results from the challenge of the skeptics. This I believe to be the case with the New Testament accounts of Jesus. The Jesus tradition has a consistency, and was evidently handled with a respect and a reverence which make it seem extraordinarily unlikely that it was fabricated or drastically modified in the generation after he lived and died.

Literary Impact

This conclusion is consistent with a judgment which may be made on purely literary grounds. The person of Jesus has captured the imagination, challenged the assumptions, and commanded the devotion of countless people down the centuries. Such a reputation could have been acquired only by a person who came over, through the accounts available to us, as credible, consistent, and true to life. A cardboard figure, an artificially constructed personality, could not have had such an effect on so many people. This impact made by Jesus down the centuries severely limits the possibilities: either his character was created by a literary genius, or else he was in reality such as he is portrayed in the gospels. But if anything is certain about the gospels as we have them, it is that none of them, nor any prototype they drew on, was primarily a literary work: it is impossible to discern the working of a mind behind them comparable, say, with that which produced the influential and enduring figure of a Hamlet or a David Copperfield. But if so, then we are driven back to the alternative: the figure presented by the gospels must actually have existed, and existed in a form that has not been materially distorted or changed by the modifications which each gospel writer may have introduced. A fabricated Jesus, or one altered out of recognition by his early followers (the "Christ of faith" as opposed to the "Jesus of history"), simply could not have made the mark on the world, both within and outside the community of believers, which has been the achievement of Jesus of Nazareth. Whether the claims implicit in the gospel narratives relative to Jesus' special authority or divine status are valid, or even whether they were made in any form by Jesus himself, is another matter. The question before us here is simply that of the reliability of the gospel accounts; and to a literary critic, at least, it may seem unreasonable to suggest that these are fraudulent or fictitious.

But it may be that by relegating the question of Jesus' claims to another discussion we are simply evading the real problem. That Jesus laid claim to a special authority and to a unique relationship with his heavenly Father is not just a small detail which we can safely leave on one side; it is at the heart of the evangelists' presentation of him. It makes no difference whether he made these claims himself or the church began to do so after his death: the only Jesus we have is one who, implicitly or explicitly, presented himself as uniquely chosen and empowered by God. To try to detach these claims from the portrait of him given in the gospels (let alone from the image of him we receive from Paul's letters) is to risk leaving nothing of substance that we can recognize as the same Jesus who has left his mark on history. If we are not disposed to accept these claims, we may find the account of Jesus unreal and incredible, in which case we must accuse the evangelists of falsifying history. And there is more: much of the gospel story consists of miracles, events which it is only rational to believe could not have happened. If the gospels report these as factual occurrences, and also present a person who made claims (such as that the Kingdom of God would come in the lifetime of his followers) which we can confidently say were false, how can we continue to respect them as historically reliable accounts?

39

Miracles

To take the question of miracles first. For the many centuries during which the truth of Scripture was accepted without question, the miracles were regarded as among the most important elements in the gospel story: if Jesus performed such deeds, are we not compelled to acknowledge his unique status and power? Precisely the opposite conclusion was drawn in a later age of scientific rationalism: if the story of Jesus was adorned with such plainly fictitious episodes, we would do better to regard them as embarrassing relics of a credulous age and concentrate on his timeless religious and ethical message. Today, neither attitude is appropriate: we cannot read the miracle stories as factual accounts of what may have happened; but at the same time we cannot dismiss them as fabrications or delusory experiences. There is no evidence that people in the time of Jesus were more credulous than we are; indeed, there are many recorded instances of thoroughgoing skepticism. On the other hand, the miracles themselves are seldom recorded as freakish occurrences, designed only to excite amazement or puzzlement. They belong within the framework of a belief that God may reveal his power in answer to prayer and initiate a totally unexpected and inexplicable train of events. This is a belief that has persisted down the ages, and not only in Christianity; and it is a belief that countless people feel has been validated by events in their own experience which they have readily called "answers to prayer" and have believed to be, in that sense, "miraculous." To reject the gospel accounts of "miracles" out of hand on rationalist grounds, or to attempt to explain them away by retelling the stories as if they were misunderstood natural occurrences (as has been a popular approach in the past — the healings were cases of psychosomatic conditions, the exorcisms were the calming of hysteria, the feedings of the multitudes were picnics to which everyone had in reality brought their own food, and so forth) is to fail to do justice to the much more nuanced attitude toward such stories that is widely prevalent today.

But there is another more fundamental reason why it is now possible to give the miracle stories more credence than in the past. Our understanding of causation has changed. We have ceased to think in terms of simple cause-and-effect. The model of understanding we inherited from David Hume, which can be represented as one cause leading to one observable effect, like balls colliding on a billiard table, certainly created a problem for the religious mind. Given the "laws of nature," which seem to determine an invariable progression from a given cause to a predictable effect, it was hard to see how God could be conceived of as both having created these laws and being willing to interfere with them to effect "miracles." But this model has now been superseded by the concept of multiple causation. Events are to be imagined, not as unique occurrences preceded by a single cause, but as the outcome of a process subject to manifold constraints and impulses. It is now widely understood that when we say "smoking causes cancer" we are not speaking of simple cause-and-effect. Smoking does *not* always "cause" cancer. We are speaking of an outcome toward which *one of the factors* is likely to be smoking. But there will have been many other factors, not all of which are even necessarily accessible to human knowledge. Among these factors the religious mind can number, without contradiction, the absence of anyone having prayed for the cancer victim. Similarly, the apparently "miraculous" recovery of a cancer patient (such as is often reported) may be understood as due to a combination of factors or "causes," one of which, it is perfectly reasonable to think, may have been the prayers offered or the religious rites administered on behalf of that person.

If this kind of analysis is applied to the gospel miracle stories, it does not of course resolve all our difficulties. However complex the causes may have been, it remains impossible (according to our present understanding) for water to be turned into wine, for half a dozen loaves to feed five thousand people, or for a person crippled from birth suddenly to stand up straight and walk. But what we have to analyze are not these physical phenomena themselves but the reports we have of them in the gospels. It is not just that something must have happened. Something was also believed to have happened, and was then told and retold in a certain way. The outcome was the story as we have it, and to produce this outcome a large number of factors will have come into play. That some kind of divine influence was present among those factors is a perfectly reasonable belief. We shall never know what actually happened; but we can be open to the possibility that something very remarkable did happen, and that among the multiple causes of the event and of the subsequent responses to it there was an element of divine intervention such that faith and understanding were strengthened and enlarged. Remove these stories from the gospels and a vital strand disappears. Keep them in view, and it becomes relevant to note the restraint with which they are told (compared with narratives of merely freakish events that have come down to us from antiquity) and the way in which, though they are a significant part of the narrative, they are not allowed to dominate it. The handling of them by the evangelists is unsensational and responsible; it is certainly not such as to prevent us from believing that the overall story they are telling is broadly "historical."

A Credible Character?

What, then, of the claims made by and for Jesus that he was in a unique relationship with God, that his teaching had supreme authority, and that he stood on the brink of a catastrophic turn in world affairs (which has never happened)? Do these claims confront us with having to decide (in G. K. Chesterton's words) that he was "bad, mad — or God"? And if we find we can accept none of these options — if, for example, we think that Jesus was good but seriously misunderstood by those who have left us records of him — are we forced to dismiss the gospels as historical accounts of Jesus? Is their presentation merely a pretentious inflation of an originally far less remarkable character, developed in the interests of promoting him to divine or semi-divine status?

It is of course true that there are clear signs in all the gospels (particularly in that of John, which is usually assumed, partly for this reason, to be the latest) of adaptations made after the event in the light of the resurrection and the subsequent faith of the church. Indeed, generations of New Testament scholars have devoted much of their time to trying to identify these "christological" modifications and additions and to distinguish them from "original" Jesus material. But even if many of the crucial formulations of Jesus' status (such as "You are the Christ, the Son of the living God," in Matthew 16.16) are regarded as evidence of the later faith of the church rather than of anything Jesus is likely to have confessed to, this does not by any means rule out finding instances of more accurate reporting.

One of the most striking features of the accounts in all three synoptic gospels (though to a lesser extent in John) is not the tendency of Jesus to lay claim to exceptional status but rather the opposite, that is, his *reserve* in the face of such claims being made about him. His favorite self-designation ("Son of man"), which significantly is almost entirely absent from any part of the New Testament except the gospels, and clearly was not an expression that was used or invented by early Christians, is one of which the precise implication still eludes us; but it was at most an oblique way of indicating that the speaker occupied a special place in the purposes of God. Similarly with "Messiah" or "Christ," a title that Jesus' followers most certainly attached to him with conviction, possibly even in his lifetime: there have been others in Jewish history (Sabbatai Tzevi, in the seventeenth century, is a notable example) who were for a time thought to be the messiah, but in each case it was others who recognized them as such, not they themselves who laid claim to the title; and Jesus seems to have conformed to this pattern. In all the gospel accounts it is others who award him the title, not Jesus who claims it; and where he assents to it, he frequently does so with a degree of reserve which is an entirely plausible attitude for him to have taken, and suggests faithful memory and reporting rather than deliberate falsification or exaggeration. In short, if we balance the alleged claims and pretensions attributed to Jesus against the reluctance he is also reported to have shown, we are confronted with a figure who need by no means be regarded as a creation of the early church, but whose genius and apparent authority were such as to raise from the very beginning the question of his relationship to God and his place in the history of his people and of the world. As accounts of the impact made by such a person, the gospels can surely claim to be taken seriously as history.

We have looked at the synoptic gospels and Acts with a view to comparing them with other historical writings of their time and assessing their claim to be offering us serious history. We have also looked at the content of these gospels, and the person of Jesus which is their subject, and argued that this is sufficiently plausible not to throw into doubt the proposition that we are dealing with reputable historical records. On the person, the teaching, and the claims of Jesus there is of course much more to be said, and we will return to it in a later chapter. But in the meantime we have been reckoning without the Fourth Gospel, which has been bound up with the other three since at least the second century C.E. In one sense, this gospel is clearly less 'historical' than the others. Does this mean that it is not reliable? And does its association with the other three contaminate their witness and cause us to think again about the historical value of all of them? This is the question to which we must next turn.

CHAPTER 3

Evaluating John

⸺∞⸺

If we find a problem in John's gospel, we are not the first to do so. As early as the second century there were Christian groups who had reservations about accepting it as authoritative on the grounds that it taught doctrines about Christ which they could not accept. Indeed, it was as obvious to the early generations of Christians as it is to us that the Fourth Gospel is *different* from the others — the often quoted words of Clement of Alexandria, that John's is a "spiritual" gospel, as opposed to the others which offer only narrative, are as good a summary as any of the general impression that this gospel has always made upon its readers. But what *is* a modern problem is that it appears less "historical": for the purpose of telling us what actually happened with regard to Jesus, as opposed to what this evangelist thought was important about him, John's gospel seems not merely different from the other three but distinctly inferior. The "quest of the historical Jesus" has normally concentrated its efforts entirely on the synoptic gospels and left the fourth largely out of account. Is this justified?

Before addressing this question directly, we must take account of the fact that from very early times — certainly by the middle of the second century — the church had come to accept that its knowledge and teaching about Jesus were based, not on a single account, but on *four*. Though the fourth might seem different from the others in certain respects, there was never any question of three plus one; there was never any tendency (before the modern period of critical study) to set it apart from the others or to regard it as a less important source of knowledge. Even the early "harmonies" of the gospels, beginning with Tatian in the second century, used sections of John's gospel alongside the other three when building up a composite account of the life of Jesus. Indeed, for Tatian the narrative of the Fourth Gospel provided the framework into which the accounts provided by the synoptics were to be fitted. Moreover, once the fourfold character had been accepted — which appears to have been quite early in the second century and to have coincided with the use by Christians of the codex format for their books (making possible the writing of more than one gospel in a single volume, which would have been impossible on a scroll) — it appears that the meaning of the word "gospel" itself precluded regarding any one of them as less important than others: "gospel" meant the message of and about Jesus Christ, which was handed on to the church in versions "according to" individual evangelists. By definition it was the same gospel, and it could be derived from any of the four; but each had presented it in a way which made it irreplaceable in the church's "canon."

This early acceptance of just four standard accounts of the life, death, and resurrection of Jesus — neither more nor less — suggests that it was not "history," in the sense of facts, dates, order of events, and biographical development, that the Christians were looking for in their gospels, but rather a telling of a story with which they were already familiar in a way that would help them to understand its meaning. To this, each gospel had its own unique contribution to make. By then, other "gospels" had come into existence, offering different narratives (or, in the case of that of Thomas, no narrative at all but a collection of sayings) and different interpretations. But a decision had been made that only four were authoritative or "canonical"; the others were excluded as liable to lead into heresy. Of these four, there was no question of one being less authoritative than the rest. True, Mark's gospel, being the shortest, and its material being almost all available in Matthew and Luke, tended to be neglected. But any citation from it would carry the same weight as one from any of the other three.

To this extent, the question of the "historical value" of the Fourth Gospel is a modern one; and in modern times it has been answered in very different ways. The uncritical reader, noting what is said about the "beloved disciple," his intimacy with Jesus, and his alleged responsibility for the truth of the gospel (all matters which, as we shall see, raise a host of critical questions) might well infer that the gospel was written by a disciple who was especially close to Jesus and whose account is therefore the most likely to approach the truth. This inference in fact lies behind the majority of the "lives" of Jesus that were written under the influence of the Romantic movement in the nineteenth century and which used the Fourth Gospel as their basic text. But the more critical approach that was stimulated by the Enlightenment and began to gather momentum toward the end of the eighteenth century dismissed the notion that the author was a disciple and assumed that the gospel was a fairly free rewriting of the story, using material from the synoptic gospels and having much theological interpretation but no new historical information to add to the others. For the next two centuries it virtually disappeared altogether from research into "the historical Jesus."

A Historical Source after All?

A further change took place in the mid-twentieth century, when the question began to be asked: If the writer of the Fourth Gospel had only the material in the other three gospels to work with, could he have completed his work? A painstaking scrutiny of all the passages which stand in any sort of parallel with sections of the other gospels, undertaken particularly by C. H. Dodd, pointed to the conclusion that this evangelist must have had some other source of information to be able to write as he did. In which case, might not this information be as ancient and reliable as that in the other gospels? And might not the Fourth Gospel therefore be after all an important source for the historical Jesus?

To take only one example: John 6.15 states that Jesus "realized that they meant to come and seize him to proclaim him king." This piece of information occurs nowhere else. May it not be a nugget of historical truth? Indeed, C. H. Dodd made it the pivot of his last book on Jesus, *The Founder of Christianity* (1971). For him, it was the key which explained much of Jesus' restrained activity and apparent reticence: he was avoiding being made king.

And this immediately raises another question. Where John's gospel actually conflicts with the others, might it be John, and not (as usually thought) the synoptics who has it right? Take one of the most obvious points of difference. In Mark (followed by Matthew and Luke) the story of Jesus has a simple structure. Act One: the ministry in Galilee, with general acceptance by the crowds. Entr'acte (greatly extended by Luke): journey to Jerusalem. Act Two: arrival in Jerusalem, rejection, and death. In John, the sequence of events is more complex. Jesus travels back and forth between Galilee and Jerusalem, attending different festivals (not just Passover) and encountering a combination of acceptance and rejection at every stage. Critical scholarship used to assume almost without question that John's order of events was artificial, constructed for the evangelist's own purposes, and that the true sequence is to be found in Mark. But is this really more likely? It was one of the solid gains of form criticism to have established that the earliest material about Jesus was remembered independently of its original context, and that the actual order of most events is lost beyond recall. Mark's arrangement, therefore, must be due to his own or some predecessor's editorial judgment; and it is certainly a scheme that is clear and easy to follow. But is it historically plausible? Would a Galilean Jew of Jesus' piety and religious pretensions have stayed away from Jerusalem and its festivals over a period of two to three years — a startling departure from the usual obligation to attend festivals whenever possible? Are there not hints even in the synoptic scheme of more than one visit — such as the episode of the cursing of the fig tree, which would make perfect sense at the autumn festival of Tabernacles but is bizarre at Passover ("It was not the season for figs," as Mark correctly observes, 13.3)? John's scheme is certainly more elaborate, and much harder to hold in the mind; but may it not stand closer to reality, as well as plausibly suggesting a more nuanced response to Jesus throughout his activity?

Take another instance. The feeding of the five thousand (or four thousand) is one of the best-attested episodes in the gospels, having given rise to no fewer than six accounts of such a miracle. In the synoptic gospels it has a simple motivation. The hour was late, the place was remote and uncultivated *(erēmos)*, and the disciples recommended that the people go off to the neighboring villages to get themselves something to eat. Instead Jesus miraculously provided bread and fish for all. By contrast, the account in John says nothing about the lateness of the hour or the remoteness of the place (other than that it was "up the hillside," *ana to oros,* 6.3), and his question, "Where are we to buy bread to provide for these people?" is explicitly said to be to "test" Philip, not to explore ways of meeting the people's needs. The only hint of motivation for the miracle that follows is in the evangelist's note, "It was near the time of Passover" — that is, the reader should have in mind the one occasion in the year when a Jewish meal took place that had a special religious significance. Jesus then proceeded to inaugurate another such meal, so giving the cue for the long discourse on heavenly food which follows. Again we may ask, Which version is more likely? Certainly the visitor today to the traditional site of the miracle — a lush green meadow near the lake, within sight of the remains of Capernaum — may well feel that the version in John is the more plausible. Not that this site has a strong claim to being authentic; but Josephus tells us that Galilee at that time was very densely populated. It would have been hard to get away to a place remote enough to create a real problem for the crowds following Jesus. Should we follow the simplistic account in the synoptic gospels, or the more subtle one in John? Or should we simply assume that by the time any of the gospels was written no one any longer knew where this episode had taken place, and that each evangelist reported it as seemed to him most plausible?

At the very least it seems that we must allow for the possibility that John's gospel may occasionally offer us otherwise unrecorded historical material about Jesus. In addition to this, there are several references to places and landmarks which suggest firsthand, or at least secondhand, knowledge. Jacob's Well, Mount Gerizim, Bethesda, the Pool of Siloam, Cana of Galilee — all these existed, and when they are described in the gospel, the description matches what is now known about them.

But here we need to be careful. There is a cautionary tale in the story of Bethesda. In the 1930s, excavations at St. Anne's church in Jerusalem uncovered what did indeed appear to be a double pool such as is described in John 5 — the "five colonnades" being best explained (as was noted by Cyril of Jerusalem in the fourth century) as a four-sided building with a fifth colonnade down the center dividing two pools. In 1936 Joachim Jeremias published an account of this in great excitement: archaeology had surely revealed the exact place described in the gospel, correctly located in a district known as Beth-zatha (or Bethesda). It was only later that doubts began to be raised. Where were the remains of the "colonnades"? Column bases are an almost invariable relic of any monumental structure involving columns, and none are to be seen on this site. However, further investigation has suggested that these pools were indeed part of a healing site, possibly associated with the pagan god Asclepius. We are left with a tantalizing ambiguity. John seems to have known that there was a pool in a certain part of Jerusalem where people went to be cured. He may even have known (though he gives no hint of it) that it was a pagan sanctuary — there was after all no place for such a thing in official Jewish religion. What perhaps he did *not* know was what it looked like; but, living in Ephesus, where there were certainly monumental pools and baths, he could well have imagined how a double pool should be arranged, and in his imagination he furnished it with colonnades. In other words, we might infer from this that John had good information about Jerusalem, but not firsthand knowledge of everything he described. If so, then as a historian he passes muster according to the standards of his time.

Or does he? We can stand with reasonable certainty on the very site where Jesus met the Samaritan woman beside Jacob's Well, where the crippled man was cured at Bethesda, or where Pilate sat during Jesus' hearing before him. John's apparent topographical accuracy makes his account extremely plausible. But this does not mean that it is true! If these episodes were imaginary, any skillful storyteller might make sure that the setting was historically correct, and we would not know the difference today. To assess the historical value of John's gospel as a record of Jesus of Nazareth we need to move beyond these background considerations and apply the same kind of test as we did in the case of the synoptics. Is the person of Jesus that emerges from his narrative consistent, plausible, and sufficiently impressive to account for the impact it has made? Or is this evangelist's own theological interpretation so pervasive that he may have radically altered or even falsified his material?

The Discourses

An essential step toward considering these questions is to study the words and discourses attributed to Jesus in this gospel, for it is here that the most obvious difference lies. Whereas in the synoptics Jesus' sayings are for the most part terse, easily memorable, and such as could have been handed down orally for some time before finally being committed to writing, in John's gospel Jesus' utterances generally take the form of long paragraphs, intricately organized and clearly betraying the hand of a writer rather than the characteristic speech forms of a preacher or a public disputant. We have already seen how, in the case of Acts, the Greek expectation that history would be recorded as a matter of words as well as of deeds was met by the introduction of set speeches put in the mouths of the apostles (and others). But we noticed also that the author of Acts did not feel free to do the same for Jesus, whose utterances in Luke's gospel have the same terseness and narrative power as in Mark and Matthew. Has John therefore taken a liberty with his material about Jesus which makes him quite different from the others and therefore — potentially at least — much less reliable as a historical source?

We must not exaggerate the difference. It is not only John who has constructed sustained discourses which Jesus could hardly have uttered as they are written or which could hardly have been remembered as they were spoken. The "apocalyptic discourse" in Mark 13 (with its telltale note, "let the reader understand") is certainly a literary compilation, whatever its origin in Jesus' activity as a prophet. Matthew's Sermon on the Mount could never have been delivered as a single sermon, and is demonstrably a compilation of teachings remembered separately. Equally, it is not the case that John records none of the kind of language and style characteristic of Jesus in the other gospels. "Destroy this temple, and in three days I will build it up again." "A prophet is without honor in his own country." "In very truth I tell you, before the cock crows, you will have denied me three times." None of these would be out of place, and in fact all of them occur in some form, in the other gospels; and Matthew and Luke both contain some words which have long been recognized as characteristically "Johannine" ("Everything is entrusted to me by my Father . . . ," Matt. 11.27; Luke 10.22), which shows that we must not draw the contrast too starkly.

But this is not to deny that there are substantial discourses in the Fourth Gospel which in both style and content are totally unlike anything we have in the other gospels. We cannot evade the question whether Jesus could ever have expressed himself in this way or whether his words could ever have been precisely recalled if he did. These discourses are certainly "literary," in the sense at least that they grow around words or concepts such as "light," "living water," "truth" — concepts which themselves are far more abstract than anything ascribed to Jesus elsewhere. The writing clearly betrays long reflection in the mind of the writer, not the spontaneous speech of a teacher, preacher, or prophet; and it achieves a literary density such that no speaker could hope to be immediately understood who expressed himself in such a way. These discourses have evidently been put into the mouth of Jesus. It is not helpful to ask whether he could ever have spoken them, since this is barely possible. But it is exceedingly important to ask whether the words as we find them in John's gospel express, in their own idiom, a message which could have been intended by Jesus.

In connection with Acts, we noted that a Greek historian would have been positively expected to give an account of words spoken as well as of deeds performed; and the usual way of doing so was to intersperse the narrative with speeches setting out the pros and cons of any particular course of action. According to this model, though he seldom used the adversarial form of debate, the author of Acts could be said to have conformed with the accepted canons of historiography. But in the case of John's gospel this model hardly applies. The speeches are seldom adversarial, even though Jesus is often in the presence of his adversaries; for the most part they are developments of a particular religious theme, such as the relationship of Jesus with his heavenly Father. The most extended of the discourses is that which fills chapters 14 to 17 and is usually called, significantly, the "Farewell Discourse" — significantly, because this points us toward a literary model. On the eve of a crisis, be it a battle or a major decision of policy or tactics, the hero of a story delivers a farewell speech, expressing his aspirations and instructing his followers how to carry on his work. There are examples in Luke's work: in his gospel, Luke uses the occasion of the "last supper" to have Jesus give some very personal instruction to his disciples; and in Acts Paul summons the elders from Ephesus to come to Miletus for a classic "farewell speech." John's "Farewell Discourse" is much more extended than these, but clearly belongs to the same *genre*.

Jesus on Trial

What of the other speeches? The clue to their style and composition may be in the underlying strategy of John to present the story of Jesus as a long-drawn-out legal contest with "the Jews." Jesus makes powerful claims for himself — that he speaks and acts with the full authority of God; and much of the argument turns on the "witnesses" he can summon to support his case — John the Baptist, the disciples, the scriptures, even God himself. Jesus' speeches are clearly designed to persuade and convince in the context of a continuing "trial." It is true that there are no answering speeches on the other side; but then the purpose is not (as it might be in a Greek work of history) to present argument and counter-argument, but to invite the reader to appreciate all that Jesus does and says as building up a cumulative case for the status and authority of Jesus. The procedure was perhaps more akin to that found in Greek biographies than in histories; but it was certainly not such as to cause the reader to impugn the author with deliberate falsification.

The prominence of the "trial" motif in this gospel has not always been recognized. This may be because the legal procedures familiar to John's Jewish contemporaries were different in significant respects from those that are familiar to us today, or indeed those that have been customary in Western civilization for many centuries. There was, for instance, no necessary line drawn between witnesses and judges: if those who claimed to have witnessed an offense were also persons with legal competence, there was no reason why they should not form part of a judicial tribunal. Moreover, these tribunals did not require the formal apparatus of courtroom and functionaries: a group of qualified experts could constitute themselves as a "court" wherever they happened to be. Accordingly, there are several occasions in John's gospel where a dispute between Jesus and "the Jews" quickly takes on a judicial character and ends in a condemnation and sentence, which only a strange quality of elusiveness in Jesus prevents from being immediately carried out. And there was another feature of the legal system which is unfamiliar to us. This is the importance of witnesses. Western proceedings place great weight on circumstantial evidence. Letters, fingerprints, spots of blood, and anything else that can be adduced in court may have a decisive influence on the verdict. But in a Jewish trial the outcome depended far more on the character of the witnesses who could be summoned in defense. If defendants could bring forward persons to speak for them who were well respected in the community, they would have a strong chance of acquittal. In John's gospel the story opens with the summoning of witnesses — John the Baptist, Nathanael — attesting that Jesus is a person of special status. But later, these "witnesses" are no longer available, creating a difficulty for Jesus when confronted by his accusers. The one witness to whom he could now appeal was God himself. But "calling God to witness" amounted to an oath, and this would have left his opponents with no choice but to accept his statements and wait to see whether God would punish him as a perjurer. In the event, Jesus did not name God; he spoke only of his "father." This let the prosecutors off the hook: not recognizing that this "father" was God, they were not forced to regard the calling of this witness as an oath and so were free to discount it. As a result, the "trial" proceeded to further accusations and rebuttals.

It follows that once we shed some of the assumptions which belong to our Western legal procedures, we can recognize that much of the story of Jesus is told in the Fourth Gospel in the form of a series of encounters with "the Jews" that take the form of episodes in a trial, challenging not just Jesus' interlocutors, but also the reader, to form a judgment about him. The nature of the charge or charges brought against him is not substantially different from those recorded in the synoptic gospels. There, though considerable offense seems to be caused by Jesus' behavior on the sabbath, the actual charges are confined to blasphemy: claiming to pronounce a man's sins forgiven (Mark 2.7), and apparently identifying himself with the Son of man soon to be glorified at the right hand of God (Matt. 26.64). In John's gospel, a healing on the sabbath results in a legal challenge (5.16). This is a departure from the synoptic account, but only to the extent that there sabbath healings cause offense and provoke hostility, while here they are said to be actually against the law and result in an attempt at prosecution. But in any case a further charge is soon added based on his apparently blasphemous claim (10.36) to have God as "his own father" (5.18), and this, in one form or another (including the mysterious statement, "Before Abraham was, I am" [8.58]), remains the substance of the dispute. The essence of the "trial" was to determine whether Jesus' claim was valid; if not, it was blasphemous and incurred the gravest penalty. This runs very close to the synoptic account.

Jesus Divine?

It is frequently said that the Christology of the Fourth Gospel (by which is meant the claim that Jesus is something more than an ordinary human being) is considerably more advanced or developed than in the other gospels. In particular, it appears that Jesus claims, or is claimed, to be divine — a claim certainly not made in the synoptics and barely hinted at even in the rest of the New Testament. But is this correct? It is certainly true that this gospel uses images and metaphors to describe Jesus' relationship with his heavenly Father which do not occur elsewhere. But these do not necessarily imply a claim that he was actually God. There has recently been some interest among scholars in the analogy of "agency," which is explicitly mentioned once in the Fourth Gospel (13.16) and arguably underlies much of the language which appears to raise Jesus to the level of his heavenly Father. In his time, the institution of agency was an important factor in commercial life, and rested on the principle that "the agent is as the one who sent him." Jesus placed much emphasis on having been "sent" by God; and this implied that when he spoke or worked (for instance, on the sabbath), it was as if God himself was present. This is what gave his disputes with "the Jews" such urgency. If they disputed the truth of what he said, they were questioning the veracity, not just of Jesus (the agent), but of God himself ("making God a liar," as the First Letter of John memorably puts it, 1.10). In other words, they were committing blasphemy. If they accepted it, they were bound to heed him and respect him as they would God — an acknowledgment finally demonstrated by Thomas who, recognizing Jesus as the fully authorized agent of God, and so finding himself in a situation in which it was as if God was present, had no option but to confess, "My Lord and my God" (20.28).

Is this a "higher" or more developed Christology? It is certainly true
that statements such as "The Father and I are one" (10.30) are hard to imagine in the mouth of a religious teacher in Palestine, where an absolute
monotheism was taken for granted, and suggests an environment where
such a concept would have caused less immediate protest. Once again we
must allow for this gospel having rephrased Jesus' meaning in a form that
drew out its implications for a somewhat different audience. Nevertheless,
it is difficult to argue that it goes so far as actually to identify Jesus with
God: it is only as God's "agent" that Jesus is given apparently divine attri-
butes. But what of Jesus' claim to have existed before Abraham (8.58)? It can
certainly be argued that this, being a claim to preexistence, goes far beyond
anything said in the synoptics. But we must remember that one of the questions posed by Jesus was whether or not he was the Messiah. If he was, then
language traditionally used of the Messiah could properly be used of him.
As we observed in chapter 1, there was a rabbinic saying (which has strong
claims to date back at least to the time of Jesus) stating that one of the
things which has existed from the moment of creation is "the name of the
Messiah." By this was presumably meant that when the Messiah came, it
would not be a kind of afterthought, as if God found that his purpose for
the world was being frustrated by human sin and foolishness and decided to
rectify things by sending a Messiah. Rather, the intervention of such a figure to introduce a new dispensation for human beings was part of God's
original creative design: the Messiah's "name" was there from the beginning.
Do the words used by Jesus necessarily mean more than this?

It is true that this is not the only respect in which the figure of Jesus
may appear different from that in the other gospels. It has been argued, for
instance, that in the Fourth Gospel Jesus, even if not actually divine, is presented as a supernatural figure, apparently floating above the constraints to
which ordinary human beings are subject, free to come and go as he pleases
despite threats to his life, performing supernatural acts of healing, trans-
forming substances (water into wine), walking on the surface of the lake,
feeding a multitude from a tiny provision of food, and claiming the power
to submit or not to submit to his enemies as he pleased. But again, the contrast with the other gospels may be overdrawn. The miracles of healing,
feeding, and walking on water are all reported in them also; and even if the

Johannine Jesus seems at times to claim a surprising freedom to choose his destiny, his story is certainly not the play-acting of a superhuman figure only pretending to be engaged in human affairs; it involves a serious and agonizing moral decision whether or not to submit to a cruel destiny, however much the suffering involved may be suffused by the conviction that it will be a means of manifesting the purposes and glory of God. Indeed, when it comes to the closing scenes of the trial and crucifixion, these, though differing in certain details from the other accounts, have the same dramatic power precisely because they depict a man caught inexorably in a series of events altogether beyond his control. At this point, though also throughout the earlier chapters, the humanity of Jesus is as little in question as in the other gospels.

There is, however, one respect in which the figure of Jesus in the Fourth Gospel is startlingly different from that in the other gospels. In the synoptics, Jesus consistently withdraws himself from the foreground in order to direct attention to God. His parables, his teaching, even his miracles, all focus, not on himself, but on his, and our, heavenly Father. When he speaks of himself at all, it is usually by means of a phrase that continues to puzzle interpreters: the Son of man. Even if, as seems likely, this was a conscious and deliberate allusion to the representative figure in Daniel 7 who takes his place at the right hand of God at the moment of divine judgment, the fact that Jesus always refers to him in the third person, and never explicitly identifies himself with him, creates an impression consistent with another well-established meaning of the phrase "Son of man." It seems that, at least in conversation, the phrase was a way of referring to oneself obliquely, as if to say, "Someone, you know who. . . ." And this would also be characteristic of Jesus. Throughout, one could say that if Jesus proclaims himself at all in the first three gospels, he does so with a reticence so remarkable that it is difficult not to believe it is an authentic memory of his characteristic manner of speech. When one turns to the Fourth Gospel, what a contrast! There Jesus devotes long paragraphs of teaching to explaining his own mission and status in relation to God, and to drawing out (by means of images such as shepherd, living water, bread from heaven, and many more that are quite absent from the other gospels) the true significance of his time in the world. Indeed, so great is the contrast that we are faced with a choice. It seems impossible that Jesus could have spoken about himself in two such profoundly different idioms. Only one of them can claim to be authentic; and we instinctively make our choice in favor of the synoptic version. In which case, what are we to say of the reporting in John's gospel? Has he seriously distorted the record of Jesus' remembered utterances, so as to give them a "Christocentric" character which would have been quite strange to Jesus' normal style? Or may we perhaps say, as before, that the evangelist was simply being faithful to the narrator's task of giving the words as well as the deeds, that is to say, of providing in Jesus' self-description the reasons for his having acted as he did? John may well have been drawing on actual memories; but if so, he refashioned them in such a way as to make more intelligible the progress of the story and its significance for future generations.

Love Your Enemies?

There is a further difference between the words of Jesus in the Fourth Gospel and in the other gospels which raises rather different issues. In the matter of moral teaching, there is a notable absence in the Fourth Gospel of specific injunctions or instances — there are none of the same parables, with their challenging impact on moral behavior, and those that are alluded to (such as the "hidden parable" of the son/apprentice in John 5.19-23) are again targeted on the person of Jesus, not on the conduct of those who hear him. Indeed, the moral teaching in this gospel is almost confined to a repeated emphasis on the primacy of love ("Greater love has no man than this . . . ," John 15.13), with the corollary that this love involves humble service to one another, such as Jesus demonstrated by washing his disciples' feet. But if we ask to whom this love should be shown, the answer seems quite unambiguous: love *one another*. That is to say, the love to be shown by Christians is a love confined within their own community. "The world" outside will hate them, and there is no suggestion that they should respond to this hatred by love. The injunction to "love your enemies" is not so much as hinted at. The message of this gospel is that the love Jesus' followers are commanded to show is towards *fellow Christians*. "The world" is to be distrusted and shunned.

Once again, the contrast with the other gospels must not be drawn too sharply. Apart from the command recorded in both Matthew and Luke to love one's enemies (which is, of course, a very big "apart"), there are only two passages in the synoptics which explicitly answer the question *whom* one should love. One is the parable or tableau of judgment in Matthew 25, where those on the left hand are accused of not having performed the traditional acts of love toward the hungry, the destitute, and the prisoners. But then we are told that these people may be described as "the least of these my brothers," which many believe is a coded way of referring to those *within the church* — in which case what is being laid upon us is the responsibility to create a community in which these acts of mercy become the norm, without any suggestion that this kind of practical love should be extended to outsiders.

The other, of course, is the parable of the Good Samaritan. This is certainly unambiguous; but it remains the only passage recommending a love that should be extended without discrimination to any fellow human being. Neither Mark's nor Matthew's gospel contains anything of the kind. It is certainly true that other parts of Jesus' teaching may be taken to imply this (and it is possible that the First Letter of John takes it in this direction, if the "brother" whom one is to love is taken to mean anyone with whom one has to do), and indeed it has been so taken in Christian tradition. But it would be hard to say that this is the implication in the Fourth Gospel, where the exercise of love appears to be distinctly sectarian: those outside the sect may, it seems, legitimately be "hated." Indeed, if the word "sect" is correct in this context, it points us in the direction of an explanation. What we are hearing is the voice of a community that is vulnerable and embattled. It has little opportunity to develop reciprocal relations with those outside; its charitable actions are of necessity inward looking, and the command to love one's enemies becomes less important than the need to maintain solidarity in the community. We may see the influence of a later phase of church life on the preservation and selection of Jesus' moral teaching, just as we may see in Matthew's gospel hints of a later church order appearing in the record of Jesus' teaching on how his followers were to relate to one another.

For many readers, accustomed to the reverential way in which the gospels, as part of "Holy Scripture," are regarded as literal mediators of the truth about Jesus, it may be difficult to come to terms with the notion that John's gospel, even more than the others, is a product, not just of original memories of Jesus, but of later reflection and interpretation in the church. This is certainly the assumption that lies behind virtually all critical commentaries on the gospels; and in the case of John's gospel there is now a scholarly consensus that it reflects conditions in the first generations of the church's existence rather than those surrounding Jesus himself, and that it can be confidently dated to the very last decades of the first century C.E. But they may legitimately ask whether they are forced to accept this conclusion. Does not John's gospel make claims, much more explicit than the others, to first-hand witness and exceptional reliability?

It is true that the consensus is rarely questioned. Nevertheless, one notable challenge, that of J. A. T. Robinson in 1976 to which we referred earlier, at least exposed the fragility of the arguments in favor of the relatively late dating; and the relevance of the principal piece of evidence (the fear of being put "out of the synagogue," John 9.22; 12.42; 16.2) is still the subject of intense debate among both Christian and Jewish scholars. It cannot be said, therefore, that a late date for the gospel, and its genesis in the tensions arising in church life some fifty to sixty years after the time of Jesus, are conclusions to which we are forced by the evidence. On the other hand, whatever else it is, this gospel is certainly not a bare record of events in the life of Jesus. From a literary point of view it shows signs of considerable skill and sophistication. However much editing and rearrangement the text may have undergone (and, as we shall see, the occasional apparent inconsistencies and illogicalities in its construction have prompted countless attempts to recover its "original" form), it is still clearly the work of a highly conscious and creative writer. It is not just that he introduces, or at least elaborates, discourses of Jesus to an extent far beyond what could possibly be regarded as accurate reports of his words; his narrative also betrays the hand of an accomplished storyteller.

This, it could be said, is to tread on dangerously subjective ground. What makes a good story, and what gives that story its power other than the events themselves, are questions notoriously difficult to answer. The claim, therefore, that we can detect the author's hand in the actual narration must be advanced cautiously. There are, however, certain fairly objective criteria that can be used.

Evaluating John

Literary Traits

One technique that was well established in Greek drama and in subsequent literature was the use of irony. When the audience or the readers know what the outcome will be, but the protagonists do not, the author has an opportunity to give the words allegedly spoken by the characters a sharp, ironical edge. Occasionally this may be explicit: Jesus speaks of the temple being destroyed and himself raising it up again in three days (2.19). His opponents can see only the literal meaning, which they naturally regard as preposterous; his disciples come to see the point only later; but the reader knows at once that this is an allusion to the resurrection, the church now being the new "temple." Or again: when the high priest speaks of Jesus' impending death as being "for the people," what was spoken as a comment on the actual situation (the necessity for a political hostage to the Romans) is said by the author to be a "prophecy" of what Jesus' death would mean "for the race" at large (11.50-52). But the technique can also be used with more subtlety. There is irony in Jesus telling the Samaritan woman to call her husband when he knows that she has had five husbands and that the man she is now living with is not her husband (4.16-18). There is irony when Jesus tells his disciples that Lazarus "has fallen asleep" when in fact he is dead but will be "awakened" by Jesus (11.11). There is irony in Jesus' saying to the Pharisees, "You will look for me, but you will not find me; and where I am you cannot come" — the Pharisees are puzzled, and wonder if he means that he will go abroad into the Diaspora, but the reader knows (or at least can guess) his real meaning. There is also irony when he talks to his disciples about being away "a little while" — the disciples are mystified, but the reader, who is deemed to know the story of the resurrection, is alert to his meaning. This trait is unique to the Fourth Gospel: the others have nothing like it. It is possible that it was characteristic of Jesus' speech, faithfully reproduced by this gospel; but it is far more likely that the writer is using a well-known technique for heightening the drama by taking his reader into his confidence about the outcome.

A still more perceptible sign of his activity as an accomplished writer is the way in which he introduces a piece of serious teaching by what might be called an "idiot question." "How can someone be born when he is old?" asks

Nicodemus (3.4), enabling Jesus to speak of the "second birth" of baptism. "You have no bucket, and the well is deep," says the Samaritan woman, giving Jesus the pretext for an explanation of the "living water" he can supply himself (4.11-14). Again, there is nothing like this in the other gospels. We are in the presence of a narrator who knows his craft. And the same goes for another stylistic feature, which might be called "leading the reader up the path." Jesus' teaching about baptism in chapter 3 takes a direction that would have been welcome to his readers in any church that was keenly drawing its boundaries over against the synagogue and the world. "No one can enter the kingdom of God without being born from water and Spirit" (3.5). But then, just when they will have felt reassured that they were right in stipulating that every adherent should be baptized, Jesus says, "The wind blows where it wills. . . . So it is with everyone who is born of the Spirit" (3.8). No human rules are valid when it is genuinely a matter of the Spirit of God! Again, when Jesus came to the tomb of Lazarus, we are told that he wept (11.35). The Jews take this as a mark of his love for his friend; the reader is led to think that he has genuinely come too late to save him. But then comes the raising of Lazarus, and we realize that these are tears, not of mourning, but of indignation at the people's lack of faith. These touches — and there are many of them — betray the hand of a skillful narrator, well equipped to enhance the drama of the story.

But was he equally skillful in the construction of the sequence of events? Scholarly study of this gospel has given much attention to the so-called *aporias* — the points at which the story seems not to hang well together, or to be interrupted by an episode that is out of place. The long discourse on heavenly bread in chapter 6 is given to the crowds on the shore of the lake (6.25); but in 6.59 we are told that "Jesus said these things in Capernaum." Again, in 7.23 Jesus asks, "Why are you indignant with me for making someone's whole body well on the sabbath?" which seems to refer to the healing episode in chapter 5 as if it had just happened, and suggests that chapter 6 is out of place. Again, halfway through the "Farewell Discourse" he says, "Come, let us go" (14.31), but then continues speaking to his disciples for three more chapters, and only then "went out with his disciples" (18.1). These and many other apparent discontinuities have given rise to numerous theories of the disturbance of the text, of composite authorship, and of (sometimes inept) editorial revisions. None of these theories has commanded general assent. In some ways it is tempting to think that the text is not as its original author intended and has suffered revisions and interpretations, perhaps by other hands. But it is equally possible to find connections and sequences which suggest the opposite. Indeed, there is nothing which makes it necessary to think that the gospel as we have it is not, in its essentials, the gospel as it was written — except, of course, for the last chapter, which certainly has the appearance of being a later addition. Moreover, considerable consistency is given to the narrative by a feature we have already noticed: the scenes which describe a confrontation between Jesus and "the Jews" and end with his apparent condemnation, only to have the execution of the sentence delayed by sometimes mysterious factors (Jesus was "not to be seen," 8.59, etc.), are presented as episodes of a long-drawn-out trial, each taking a stage further the issue of who Jesus really is. The very consistency of this pattern is a strong argument in favor of the scenes having been intended to stand in the order in which they now appear rather than to have been rearranged by a subsequent editor.

Historical Credentials

If, then, we follow this path, and assume that what we are reading is essentially what an individual author intended us to read, can we return to the question of how far this author mediates to us a narrative about Jesus that is consistent in itself, is compatible with the other gospels, and offers a reliable source of knowledge? Of all the gospels it is the one in which the author comes most clearly out of the shadows and appears to make statements about himself (or at least permits them to be made) which attest his authority and reliability. The "beloved disciple" is specifically said to have been intimate with Jesus, to have been close to him at the last supper, and to have been one of the first witnesses of the resurrection. This disciple is claimed as one who "vouches for what is written" in the gospel.

Does this give the Fourth Gospel a special authenticity? Certainly these words could not have been written unless the writer (or whoever, at least, wrote chapter 21) believed that they reinforced the claim of the gospel to be true. But this, of course, does not take us much further. Even if he believed this, it may not have been the case. It is not clear from his words *how much* of the gospel he was referring to — all of it, part of it, or just chapter 21. And, in any case, "the beloved disciple" may be a fiction, a representative figure, standing for the disciples in general (whom Jesus certainly "loved," 13.1) or for those who came after and were conscious of the same love. None of this makes a case for a special claim on historical truth or accuracy, any more than the "eyewitness" who saw blood and water issuing from Jesus' side on the cross and vouched for the truth of his report — as any visitor to a law court knows, by no means all "eyewitnesses" stand up to cross-examination! Indeed, one could argue the opposite: at this point the author protests too much, trying to encourage belief in an unbelievable event by invoking eyewitnesses.

In short, we shall not make much progress if we try to establish this gospel's historical credentials by citing its references to an eyewitness or a beloved disciple. We can judge that the account it gives of Jesus is plausible as far as the main course of events is concerned — perhaps, as we have seen, more plausible in some respects than that in the other gospels. We can readily admit that within this framework the author has taken considerable liberties in arranging the material so as to emphasize the forensic aspects of the disputes between Jesus and his opponents; and we can allow for his having made exceptionally generous use of the convention to provide a rationale of the action through carefully written discourses attributed to the main character. We must recognize that he has presented a Jesus who speaks in a different idiom, who focuses attention on himself to a unique degree, who interprets the significance of the future in a quite different way ("eternal life" is not merely a condition to be hoped for after death but a possession that may be grasped in the present), and whose moral teaching appears to reflect the ethos of a relatively closed community compared with the wider reach of, say, the parable of the Good Samaritan. But we must also recognize that the synoptic gospels, and doubtless the tradition lying behind them, also bring their own interpretation to the facts about Jesus, and that many of these differences between the gospels are less about the facts than about the interpretation. It is as a different and complementary interpretation of these facts that the church has always accommodated this gospel alongside the others. That the interpretation, and some of the facts, are at such variance with the first three gospels has in recent times been thought to be fatal to the gospel's essential reliability. Powerful arguments can be marshaled to support this view, and none of the counterarguments advanced in this chapter may be robust enough to refute them. Yet they are by no means conclusive; and it can hardly be said that we are forced by modern critical study to form an opinion of the gospel fundamentally different from that which has been held for the greater part of the history of the church.

CHAPTER 4

Seeking a Moral Compass

———— ∞∞∞ ————

D oes the New Testament give us reliable and authoritative moral guidance? It certainly purports to do so. Substantial sections of Paul's letters are devoted to moral exhortation, seeking to bring the moral standards of his converts up to the level to be expected in the adherents of a new religion. Much of his argumentation is directed toward moral issues on which his readers were divided, and to resolve them he drew on a range of sources for moral judgment which sometimes explicitly included references to what he believed Jesus, "the Lord," either had taught or would have approved, but which more often consisted of either biblical precedents or generally accepted moral standards. As for Jesus himself, there can be no question but that he was a teacher of morals as well as of religion (if we can make that distinction), and that he shared the ambition of all moral teachers to help his hearers live better lives. It is no surprise, therefore, that people have constantly turned to the New Testament, not just to enlarge their moral vision by adding a religious dimension to their moral thinking, but to provide guidance on the solution of particular moral problems — which is where all the trouble begins.

A Shared Heritage

For over a thousand years a popular manual of moral conduct in Christian schools and monasteries was a Greek poem, 230 lines long, attributed to a poet of the sixth century B.C.E. known as Phocylides. It contains a long sequence of maxims and aphorisms, along with a few more discursive passages, in a lively and attractive style, and was highly valued as a store of admirable moral sentiments, apparently deriving from one of the sages of ancient times. But in 1606 the distinguished scholar Joseph Scaliger demonstrated beyond all argument that the poem could not have been written at such an early date. Admittedly it employs an archaic dialect very much like that of the original Phocylides; but it has clear allusions to the Old Testament in its Greek version (and also to Stoic philosophy, as was demonstrated more recently), and betrays the hand of a much later Jewish, or conceivably even Christian, author. We need not follow the intricacies of the subsequent scholarly debate over authorship and provenance; the consensus now is that the author was a Jew around the first century of our era, anxious to promote a high standard of moral conduct; but he did this in such a way as to disguise his reliance on the Old Testament and to appeal to a wider readership than his fellow Jews. He possibly even hoped to strengthen the case of those who argued (and there were not a few who did so) that even the ancient Greek poets and teachers ultimately derived their wisdom, like the Jews themselves, from Moses. Consequently he was careful to omit any specifically Jewish rules of conduct, such as sabbath observance or circumcision, so that the poem could plausibly be ascribed to the archaic Greek author whose style he was successfully imitating, and so that his moral exhortations could be used for guidance throughout the civilized world. This is exactly what happened: it was readily adopted as a textbook of morality by Christian schools throughout the Middle Ages until the stratagem was rumbled by one of the first great Renaissance scholars. Thereafter the poem became universally known as "Pseudo-Phocylides."

The story is instructive in that it vividly illustrates the extent to which there was a shared tradition of moral teaching throughout the ancient world, drawn on alike by Jews, Greeks, and Romans — and indeed, on occasion, by Jesus himself, whose proverbial sayings ("Do not cast your pearls before swine," "The workman is worthy of his hire," "It is more blessed to give than to receive") draw on the same rich store of conventional moral wisdom, even though other parts of his teaching have a radically different character. The same tradition was duly inherited by the Christian church, which found in "Phocylides" a valuable resource for promoting high moral standards among its members. The fact that it was believed to be the work of a poet who lived five centuries before Christ was no objection; it simply showed that God had revealed the moral standards to be observed by human beings long before they were decisively endorsed by Jesus Christ, whether directly through Moses or indirectly through pagan poets.

In this respect things are not very different today. If we want to know by what moral example we should fashion our lives, or what decision we should take on a particular issue which we sincerely believe to be morally right, we can consult an almost infinite number of guides. We can read the lives of men and women whom we find to be admirable, and try to model our conduct on theirs; we can rely on the principles inculcated by our teachers when we were young and assume that our conscience is well enough formed to enable us to make the right decisions without further inquiry; we can thumb through the aphorisms of Solon or Socrates, Confucius or Pascal, Mao Tse-tung or Ghabril's "Prophet" until we find something that seems to resonate with our condition and encourages us to adopt one attitude toward life or one course of action rather than another; we can study moral philosophy and seek to uncover the rational principles that should inform our conduct; we can make a psychological investigation into ourselves to identify the unconscious influences on our thought processes and take steps to liberate ourselves from them so as to recover what we might claim to be our moral autonomy. But in all these explorations we retain absolute freedom to pick and choose. It is we ourselves who judge the value of what we find and decide what or whom to follow for guidance. Even when our conscience seems to tell us with absolute clarity what is right or wrong in a particular case, we may still be open to persuasion by arguments or influences that make us change our minds. Later still, we may come across a person who, by personal contact or through the pages of a book, makes us feel that we were wrong or else confirms us in our conviction that we were right. Yet the ultimate judgment rests always in our own hands.

"The Bible Says . . ."

It is when we bring something we call "Holy Scripture" into it that the moral argument assumes a different character. If we are Christian believers, we cannot browse in the scattered teachings of Jesus and Paul as we might in those of Gandhi or "The Prophet," and decide which, if any, we are going to take to heart. We come to our Scriptures in the expectation that they will give us, not just moral guidance, but authoritative direction as to the character we should seek to form in ourselves and the decisions we shall be called upon to make. We shall be challenged, that is to say, not just to look for gems of moral wisdom in them, but to "obey" them — that is, to accept them as, in this sense, authoritative. That is how they have in fact been accepted throughout Christian history until now. The question is, Can we, or should we, continue to do so?

There are at least three very obvious reasons why we may have doubts. The first is the Bible's apparent tendency toward self-contradiction. In one place, the people of Israel are told to be ruthless in the application of justice; in another they are told to heap coals of fire on an enemy. Paul quotes Jesus' apparently unconditional prohibition of divorce, yet he also recommends an exception in the case of marriage with an unbeliever. Jesus normally seems to preach total nonresistance, yet in Gethsemane he tells his disciples to equip themselves with swords. Jesus' teaching on love seems to be all-embracing; yet he also tells us to "hate" members of our family. How can we construct a moral code on such uncertain foundations?

The second reason is that in modern times we are confronted by questions which raise serious ethical issues but which were not envisaged by the biblical writers. Even if we accept the Bible's authority on questions to which it clearly does apply (such as sexual morality or the duty not to steal), we shall be left with a large number of other questions (the rights and wrongs of artificial insemination, nuclear deterrence, intellectual property, and a host of others) for which we shall have to find criteria outside the Bible; and once we do that, we lay ourselves open to the charge of adopting a double standard, one based on Scripture, the other on principles of our own devising.

The third reason, which may be the one which carries most weight for many people, is that history shows the ease with which the Bible may be called in evidence to support views, policies, and actions which we now recognize to be profoundly immoral. Scriptural texts have been freely used to support slavery, apartheid, and many forms of racial or sexual discrimination. Were we to accept unquestioningly the authority of these texts, we should find ourselves resisting changes and reforms which have been promoted, as often as not, on the basis of widely recognized Christian principles. Are we really to pay more attention to certain highly restrictive and (some would say) anachronistic texts than to the hard-won principles of human rights, equality between human beings, and respect for human dignity? Can there be such a thing as "biblical morality," or Christian morality based on Scripture, if it leads to conclusions clearly at variance with principles normally judged to be morally unassailable?

General Guidelines

There can be no doubt that a slavish and literal adherence to the letter of biblical commandments and exhortations will have to face objections of this kind. But these are not the grounds on which biblical authority in moral matters is usually argued for. It can be claimed, not that specific texts give an authoritative answer to specific moral questions, but that the Bible as a whole, and the New Testament in particular, furnishes the principles on which we can build an authentically Christian morality. To love your neighbor as yourself is offered by both St. Paul (Rom. 13.9) and the author of the letter of James (2.8) as a summary of all law and all morality; and it can be argued that in essentials all Christian conduct can be derived from this principle — just as, when paired with the parallel command to love God, it was proposed by Jesus as a summary of all religion as well as morality ("the law and the prophets," Matt. 22.40). In that case, may not the New Testament best be understood, not as offering a specific code of conduct, but as providing a collection of examples of how these general principles may work out in practice?

The trouble, of course, with general principles is that they are just that — general. And these ones are indeed so general that they may not be found

71

to have much cash value in the face of specific moral quandaries. When Immanuel Kant propounded his "categorical imperative" — *"Act only on that maxim whereby thou canst at the same time will that it should become a universal law"* — he was saying something very close to Jesus' Golden Rule — "Do to others as you would wish them to do to you." But there is a difference. Kant's principle is severely rational; indeed, it is at the heart of a great deal of moral philosophy. Human society is made possible precisely by the willingness of its members to consider the consequences of their actions and avoid those which, if widely imitated, would lead to a breakdown of social and commercial life. If everyone lied or stole, normal social and economic relationships would become impossible; for this reason we can all see that these actions are wrong and that we should conform to what have been established as socially beneficial principles. But this "imperative" takes one only a certain distance. It suffers from its very generality, and it is not difficult to conform to. One can avoid lying and stealing without too much trouble. But it is far from offering comprehensive moral guidance. Indeed, it may represent a kind of calculation: by observing Kant's principle, I am acting in my own interest because I need a society in which these basic standards of honesty are maintained. I shall do better, at least in the long run, if I abide by them myself than if I seek to take advantage of others' compliance with them in order to disregard them myself. The principle is in fact closer to the negative form of the Golden Rule (which is attributed to a number of moral teachers): "Do not do to others what you would not wish them to do to you." Otherwise (the implication is) they are liable to do it to you. It is much better to be on the safe side. But again, this does not take one very far. There is a great deal of what would be regarded as immoral behavior which I may feel I can safely perform because no one need ever know anything about it and there is no risk that others will do it to me in return. The principle is just too general. There is nothing specific that it tells me to do or not to do. It involves no more than a bare minimum of respect for generally accepted standards. It provides no blueprint for leading a genuinely moral life.

By contrast, consider Jesus' positive form of the Golden Rule. It is often said that it comes to the same thing as the negative form, and therefore that there is nothing original or distinctive about it. But this may not be so. As we have seen, implied by the negative form of the rule is a kind of bargain or contract: do not do what you would not wish others to do to you, *for otherwise* you may find them doing such things to you. But Jesus' positive form does not fit into this scheme at all. Do to others as you wish they would do to you, for *otherwise* — but there is no "otherwise"! No one ever thought that others *would* do to one all that one would wish them to. The world is not like that. The rule in this positive form is not a kind of contract with society. You could never calculate what you ought to do by the good things you hope others might do to you, because the chances are they will not do them. Instead it offers you, not a "rule" at all, but a new standard for your behavior *regardless* of how others may respond. It is not about calculation. It is about generosity. And there can be no such thing as a "rule" of generosity.

"What More Should I Do?"

But it follows that if this is the character of Jesus' teaching — that of general exhortations to cultivate such virtues as generosity — we can hardly look to it for guidance regarding specific moral issues. Such teaching would hardly qualify as a "moral code," nor would we be able to appeal to it when we want to determine whether a particular course of action is right or wrong. We could say, "It's not very generous to do that," but this need not mean that it is actually wrong to do it. We must surely ask, Does not the New Testament — indeed, the Bible as a whole — give us clearer guidance than that?

Of course it does. For a start, the entire Bible implicitly recognizes the force of the Ten Commandments, which are both highly specific (stealing and perjuring oneself are not just reprehensible, they are criminal offenses) and virtually universal (except for the command to keep the sabbath holy, which is a tenet of Jewish religion rather than of universal morality). These, certainly, offer guidelines for moral behavior. But again, though they are more specific, they still do not take us very far. When Jesus, in his conversation with the rich inquirer (Mark 10.17-22), reminded him of them, the man very reasonably claimed to have kept them all "from his youth up." The same would be true of the great majority of law-abiding citizens. Thus, when the man went on to inquire, "What more should I do?" he was asking for some further standards by which he could measure himself, not merely as law-abiding, but as *good* — by adopting a more generous standard of almsgiving, for example, which was indeed the kind of advice moral teachers were expected to give. A fifth of capital and a fifth of income was the suggested level of giving recommended by some of Jesus' near contemporaries. What would Jesus recommend? To his dismay, Jesus recommended what seemed impossible: giving away *everything* — and Christian interpreters and moralists have wrestled ever since with the implications of Jesus' uncompromising reply. One thing is certain: this was not a moral "rule." On this occasion at least — and there were many similar ones — Jesus responded to such questions, not with moral advice or a moral ruling, but with a highly personal challenge.

At the very least, the effect of this short dialogue with the rich inquirer was to draw attention to the inadequacy of a set of legal prohibitions when what was being asked for was a blueprint for the moral life. This, of course, was already a controversial matter. Ever since Plato there had been a debate whether a system of laws, besides establishing law and order and punishing offenders, could actually make people behave better. In Jewish culture an answer seemed to be given by the fact that a great deal in the Law of Moses consisted of what we would now call moral exhortation rather than legal definition. Even the Ten Commandments contain the clause, "Thou shalt not covet," which is a prohibition that could never be incorporated in any legal code. And there is a great deal more besides which we recognize as belonging to the project of raising the moral standards of the community rather than to the realm of legal compulsion and prohibition. Much learned discussion, in Jesus' time and afterward, was devoted to the interpretation of this written and (because God-given) unalterable law so as to make it yield directives for a truly moral and God-fearing life. Jesus stood in the same tradition. The so-called "antitheses" in the Sermon on the Mount — "It has been said, . . . but I say to you . . ." — are best understood, not as corrections or adjustments to law, but as admonitions to go far further than law could ever take you in the direction of truly moral conduct. Law is not abrogated or disregarded; but it is shown to be inadequate as a guide to virtuous and godly living.

Not that even the Jewish law was regarded as the only source of moral guidance, or even as a sufficient one. The moral character of the Jewish people was molded also by the prophets' insistence on justice and mercy and by the rich store of proverbial wisdom which the Jews shared with other cultures. It was the prophets, certainly, who saw most clearly the limitations of law and the danger of relying on it to regulate private and public relationships: they knew how easily it could be evaded by the unscrupulous and perverted for their own interests, and they called tirelessly for the recognition of overriding standards of justice, integrity, and compassion. But these were not the foundations on which any moral code could be erected. The prophets' message was not so much a prescription as a challenge, one that found a response in many of the psalms and thereby entered the moral consciousness of devout people.

Equally, no set of moral rules can be inferred from proverbial wisdom. Proverbs are distillations of generations of experience, interpreted in the light of a conviction that the human environment is more friendly than hostile and that virtuous conduct is more often rewarded than penalized. "Every cloud has a silver lining" is not always true; but it is true often enough to carry one through dark periods and expresses a basic optimism in the face of often unpromising circumstances. "Honesty is the best policy" seems often to be challenged by the apparent success of dishonest practitioners, yet it remains the conviction of the majority and thereby makes commercial activity possible. Certain dishonest actions can of course be made legal offenses and punished; but there can be no law against dishonesty itself.

It is for moral teachers to inculcate honesty by example and exhortation and by strengthening public disapproval of dishonest behavior. This is not a matter of rules. It is a matter of challenge and persuasion. Jesus certainly made use of other resources in the project of moral reform. He appealed to the law, and he endorsed and added to the tradition of proverbial wisdom ("Agree with your adversary quickly," "Do not cast your pearls before swine," and more of the same kind). But his distinctive and most lasting contribution to ethics was his radical challenge to reexamine motives and extend moral possibilities. His followers were to fashion a lifestyle, not limiting themselves to what was simply law-abiding, nor following the essentially prudential nostrums of conventional wisdom expressed in proverbs, but in the spirit of a prophetic zeal for justice, peace, and mercy and with a radical lack of self-regard appropriate to the dawning of a new era in human relationships, the Kingdom of God. Such teaching and such leadership could never be reduced to a set of laws or rules, and it has inevitably been found more inspirational than practical. When facing the hard moral decisions of daily life, Christians have found themselves turning to more systematic sources of moral guidance.

Substantial parts of Paul's letters are devoted to filling this gap. It is often remarked that actual allusions or references to Jesus' teaching are very rare (and it is not certain, though it seems probable, that even the apparently distinctive ethical demands of Romans 12 or 1 Corinthians 6 derive from Jesus); but Paul's purpose in writing was to help his readers find their way amid the moral complexities of their lives at the same time as they responded to the demands of their new faith. In doing so, he was confronting a particularly challenging situation. It was integral to Paul's understanding of the gospel that Jesus' followers should no longer be forced into conformity with the rules and standards of a Jewish community, punctiliously observing their distinctive practices ("the observances of the law"). The consequence of this was that they were thereby deprived of a clear moral code by which their community could be recognized. They needed to know how their conduct should be fashioned so as to be seen as a genuine response to moral standards at least as demanding as those of their Jewish forebears or of their pagan neighbors. Certain issues inevitably demanded settling in a way that would become accepted for their society: What should be their rules for marriage and divorce? How should they regulate their sexual desires? How far should they comply with the social demands of the pagan authorities under which they lived? On these issues Paul found himself obliged to give guidance; and he responded by offering the few actual laws or rules that can be found anywhere in the New Testament — just as Jesus had apparently responded to the question of divorce put to him as a test question by the Pharisees.

Code or Compass?

Christians have been struggling to come to terms with these laws or community rules ever since, and have done so in a rich variety of ways. The rules for divorce and remarriage within the church, and for the sexual relationships of its members, have gone through many different interpretations down the centuries and have once again become a sensitive issue today. The question which is of concern to us here is that of the authority of these rules. They occur in Scripture; and that is enough for many Christians. But given that these rules seem confined to one fairly small area of moral conduct, and that they were formulated by Paul, not by Jesus, and in a specific cultural situation; given that they are not characteristic of the moral teaching of Jesus himself (only one of whose pronouncements, that on divorce, falls into this category, and even this is reported in the gospels in different forms, once as an absolute rule, once as allowing for exceptions); given also that any attempt to find "laws" for the Christian community in the Bible runs into the difficulty that there are laws in the Old Testament which can certainly not be adhered to by Christians today — are we justified in thinking that the mere presence of these few specific injunctions in one part of the New Testament is sufficient to convert Scripture into a moral rulebook such that it can be used to make quasi-legal judgments binding on the conduct of Christians today?

This has certainly not been the view of the majority of Christians for the greater part of the history of the church. Until recently, the dominant tradition of moral theology in the Western church has been based, not on biblical teaching, but on principles derived from "natural law." Not that this was what we would now call a "secular" foundation: throughout the Middle Ages natural law, even if its origins could be traced back to Stoic philosophy, was understood as a revelation by God to human beings of their true nature and of the conduct which was appropriate to it. From a proper understanding of this divinely given nature it was believed possible to deduce moral rules, and since much of the moral teaching in Paul's epistles and elsewhere is similarly Stoic in character, it is no surprise that these rules were found to be in harmony with much of the moral teaching of the New Testament. Only the more radical of Jesus' demands, such as loving one's enemy or giving away one's possessions, went beyond these generally accepted moral norms and were accordingly thought to apply to especially dedicated Christians such as monks and nuns. For the rest, the moral standards expected were those that seemed securely based on a correct understanding of human nature under God — an approach that is still followed in the official teaching of the Roman Catholic Church: the controversial encyclical of 1968 *(Humanae Vitae)* that outlawed any form of artificial contraception was based entirely on natural-law arguments.

It is significant that according to this tradition the guidance that is offered to the Christian is expressed in terms of *law*. Law defines what is or is not permissible, what "rights" belong to a citizen, and what actions (or sometimes intentions) are not tolerated by society and are therefore punishable. A code of law that is promulgated by a particular state, though it may overlap with natural law to a great extent, will be the product of particular circumstances and may be influenced by the interests of particular classes of citizens; it cannot claim to define what is "right" or "wrong" absolutely — moralists have always insisted that law and morality are two different things. But since "natural law" is derived from an analysis of the nature of rational human beings in general, it follows that what it permits and what it prohibits may be regarded as a reliable guide to what is absolutely right or wrong. And since determining what is right or wrong is (it is assumed) the fundamental task of all moral thinking, it must hold ultimate authority, for Christians as for anyone else. There is no need to consult the New Testament or any other sacred book to discover what one ought or ought not to do; but if one does so, one will find that it endorses and corroborates the divinely given laws that are deducible from human rationality and are already present, or at least latent, in the conscience of all human beings, and provides further confirmation that to behave in the way prescribed by a rational nature is also to behave according to the will of God.

But is the distinction between right and wrong necessarily at the heart of all morality? It certainly was not thought to be so in the time of Christ, and indeed for more than a thousand years the Christian ethic was presented in quite different terms. Very broadly, one might say that until around the fourteenth century the concern of Christian moralists was not so much to distinguish between what is right and what is wrong as to lay out the path to follow in pursuit of what is good. This will, of course, involve abiding by the law — this was the first requirement Jesus demanded of the rich inquirer. But the same inquirer was not asking for a further set of laws or rules; he was asking what sort of conduct would lead to "eternal life." And the answer to questions of this kind, ever since the time of Aristotle, had been in terms of the moral dispositions and aspirations of the individual — in Matthew's version of the story, Jesus' reply was not, "If you want to have some more rules to keep," but "If you want to be perfect" (19.21). The good life, in other words, was not described in terms of success in faithfully observing a moral code but of cultivating the habits and virtues in such a way that a person's whole character would be molded by its sustained purpose of achieving happiness, promoting the common good, and conforming to the will of a loving God. And for this project the teaching of Jesus provided exceptionally apt resources. It encouraged his followers to raise their sights to new levels of moral achievement and to exercise an uncalculating generosity to a degree that left behind all prudential calculation or preoccupation with the exact extent of specific obligations. From this perspective the elaboration of law has little relevance. As Paul commented, all other laws are summed up in "You shall love your neighbor as yourself. . . . love is the fulfillment of the law" (Rom. 13.9-10). Distinctions between right and wrong have no place in the argument.

That is not to say that Christians are expected to be content with an overarching moral principle and to work out every course of action for themselves. Christianity. like all great religions, offers more specific guidance than this. It is true that the greater part of Jesus' teaching is parabolic, illustrative, challenging his hearers to draw their own conclusions and measure their conduct by the exacting standard he proposed. Yet in some instances his injunctions were quite specific. "Agree with your adversary quickly"; "Forgive your brother seventy times seven times"; "Do not swear at all." Even these, however, hardly amounted to a set of rules or a code of law. He was not saying that it is wrong, or a sin, not to obey them. Rather, "If anyone wishes to be my disciple . . ." — these were the conditions which had to be fulfilled. But the church is essentially the community of those who do wish to be his disciples, and from the very beginning it needed to help its members to see how these conditions worked out in practice and to give guidance in specific areas of moral conduct. Hence the many injunctions in the letters of the New Testament which together offer something of a moral code for the Christian to follow, and which were originally drawn, as we have seen, from a widely shared tradition of moral teaching, both Jewish and pagan.

The way this material has been used and observed in the church has varied considerably over the centuries. For St. Augustine, for example, it represented a summary of the aspirations a Christian should have in order to respond ever more faithfully to the challenge of Jesus. His moral instruction to his hearers and readers was not so much (as it is for many today) in terms of distinguishing what is right or wrong as of setting before them the goal of a perfect love for God and fellow human beings, recognizing the inherited propensity common to us all toward sinful rebellion against God and toward yielding to baser desires and impulses, but countering this with the reality of repentance and the inexhaustible possibilities of discipleship made available to every sinner by the grace of God. The same emphasis on happiness and fulfillment as the goal of a human life in conformity with the will of God was inherited by Aquinas, who enriched it with Aristotelian moral philosophy and subsequently developed it in the direction of setting Christian morality firmly in the framework of obedience to natural law and of total commitment to love of God and love of neighbor.

But at the same time there was another, less liberating consequence of the Augustinian emphasis on the fundamental sinfulness of human beings. This was the growth in the early Middle Ages of the practice of individual confession before a priest for the purpose of receiving God's forgiveness, not for sinfulness in general, but for particular sins as they were committed. To prepare them for this function, priests were provided with manuals enabling them to identify individual sins, to assess their gravity, and prescribe appropriate penances. Hence arose the necessity to classify moral conduct according to a strict code: every sin was graded according to its seriousness and allotted its appropriate penance, with an ultimate sanction of excommunication and exclusion from the church. In due course this procedure became formalized in a system of "canon law" that laid down very precisely what is and is not permissible for a Christian to do, equipped with the sanction (greatly feared, since it threatened eternal damnation) of exclusion from the sacraments and excommunication. From this it could easily be inferred that being a Christian involves obedience to a system of law; and since this law, though for the most part not actually derived from Scripture, was usually illustrated by scriptural texts that seemed to confirm it, the faithful could be excused for assuming that the Bible itself had the same legal and prescriptive character. Meanwhile, around the fourteenth century, the philosophical movement known as Nominalism caused a revolution in moral thinking that has lasted to this day: instead of encouraging the pursuit of happiness, the common good, and the contemplation of divine reality, moral philosophy became preoccupied with establishing that acts, rather than people, were good or bad in themselves, from which it followed that the most important task for moralists was not to work out the good to which human beings should aspire but to distinguish between right and wrong and identify those forms of conduct that must be avoided at any cost. For this purpose, Scripture seemed well adapted since it contains a large number of apparent prohibitions. What it tells us not to do must therefore be "wrong." Avoiding such actions is "right."

These are no more than examples of different ways in which the ethical material in the Bible has been used over the centuries. At times it has been regarded as what we might call inspirational, challenging the Christian to allow the principle of love to inform all areas of conduct; at times it has been used as a rule book, providing criteria for defining what conduct is acceptable in the church; and at times, again, it has been wrestled with as apparently performing both functions, on the one hand — especially in such passages as the Sermon on the Mount — setting a standard of self-sacrificial service that is barely possible to attain, on the other hand — both in the Old Testament and in certain passages in Paul's letters — offering rules of conduct that must be assumed to embody the ordinances of God and must therefore be observed to the letter by every member of the church. The tension between these two uses of Scripture lies behind much of the disagreement that has been characteristic of Christian moral thinking down the centuries.

Divorce and Sex

There is one area in which this tension has always been apparent, that of marriage, divorce, and sexual conduct in general. In this area the problem is caused by the social consequences of misdemeanors which are inevitably public and which may not be easily remedied. Any Christian community is likely to contain "sinners" — that is, people guilty not just of character faults such as pride but of actual offenses against others in the form of dishonest dealing, perjury, theft, slander, or indeed a whole range of acts deemed criminal under the law of the country. Sometimes they are merely suspected of wrongdoing, and the church will feel no obligation to pursue the matter publicly. At others they may be brought to trial and convicted in criminal courts. Their due punishment is prescribed and inflicted by the state; but their spiritual health may be restored by suitable penance, recommended privately by a priest, carried out in the secrecy of personal devotions, and leading to restoration among the faithful. Thus the theological affirmation that the church is "a community of sinners" is validated not just in the sense of sin which believers carry simply as human beings but also in the sinful activity of some of its members which leads them into conflict with the law. The reality of this sinfulness is not denied and indeed may be a matter of public concern, but the possibility of repentance and restoration is offered to every sinner, regardless of the gravity of the offense.

But the case is different when it comes to sexual relationships. Adultery is universally regarded as a serious offense. In Mosaic law it was, at least theoretically, punishable by death. It may result in lasting damage, not only to a marriage, but to second and third parties. Can an adulterer be "forgiven" if he or she has followed up the adulterous relationship with divorce and a second marriage? In such circumstances "repentance" clearly has little meaning: were the offense repented of, the new relationship would have to be broken off, and all thought of second marriage abandoned. But the offended spouse may not be willing to have the offender back, the new partner may not let the adulterer go, the resulting union may turn out to be permanent, happy, and "blessed." The church is then in a dilemma. Must such people be permanently excluded, whatever their promises of faithfulness and rectitude from now on, in order to show that church people regard adultery as a particularly grave sin? Or should not the fundamental Christian conviction that the grace of God is offered to any sinner in response to genuine penitence take preference over the need to present a consistent moral stance to the world? If the church is indeed a "community of sinners," should not this "sin" be treated like the others, not as a bar to membership, but as an offense to be accepted and expunged through the mercy of God, mediated through the rites of the church, and experienced in the life of grace?

The tension between these alternatives has prompted different responses by the churches throughout their history. The Roman Catholic Church has consistently refused to accept the possibility of divorced and remarried persons remaining full members and having access to the sacraments. The Orthodox Churches have always allowed remarriage (under certain conditions) at least once. The Reformed Churches have tended to be liberal. And the Church of England, after a period of rigidity, is now content to leave the matter to the discretion of the parish priest, who must only be convinced that the parties accept responsibility and feel due remorse for the breakdown of a previous marriage. Behind this variety of practice lies uncertainty about what Scripture actually enjoins. Jesus' apparent prohibition of divorce and remarriage (which are equivalent, he seems to say, to the very serious offense of adultery) has been taken as a rewriting of the Law (for divorce was legally permissible, and indeed much practiced, in his culture), as an aspiration to be taken to heart by his followers, or as a characteristic example of his tendency to sharpen his teaching by exaggeration; and the few relevant passages in Paul's letters are equally ambivalent: Paul appears to cite Jesus' prohibition with approval, but then goes on to suggest exceptions to it as if it is not universally binding. In short, it seems that the different positions which Christians have taken on the issue may always appeal to Scripture; but their scriptural basis turns out to be questionable and precarious in view of different possible interpretations of the relevant texts.

But this raises a more fundamental question, and one that seems unfortunately to be ignored even in this age when the authority of Scripture in such matters is widely challenged — and ignoring it is particularly unfortunate in the matter of attitudes to homosexual acts and dispositions which is a cause of acute disagreement among Christians today. We have seen that the characteristic style of Jesus' moral teaching was not to lay down rules that must be followed by all, but to present a challenge to raise one's sights higher in moral behavior and accept the implications of acting with radical generosity and self-sacrifice. We have seen also that the moral teaching of Paul and the other New Testament letter writers, though it occasionally reflects Jesus' radical stance, is for the most part a distillation of moral standards already accepted as admirable in the societies in which they live, and takes the form of exhortation rather than legislation. Amidst all this material, which is in the nature of answering the question that was put to Jesus, "What more must I do?" occur just a very few instances which have the form (though not necessarily the function) of specific laws or rules, and these are almost entirely concerned with sexual behavior. If Scripture is indeed to prove itself as a guide to morality, and if we are to entrust ourselves to its guidance when we seek to fashion our lives according to the will of God for each of us, must we not first come to a decision whether it should be regarded as a compendium of rules to be strictly observed or a collection of teachings intended to exhort and inspire us toward setting ourselves higher moral standards and subjecting ourselves to the discipline required to attain them? To assume (as most of us do) the second, but in the particular questions of divorce and homosexuality to treat it as the first, seems not merely inconsistent but entirely unreasonable.

The Teaching in Context

I have used the words "a collection of teachings intended to exhort and inspire. . . ." Does not such a description immediately demolish any claim that Scripture is uniquely authoritative and a reliable guide to right conduct? It is, after all, one that could be used of any number of moral treatises and devotional writings, from which, as we said at the beginning, we feel free to pick and choose those elements which seem to speak best to our personal condition. But the teaching of Jesus, and its subsequent embodiment in the beliefs and conduct of Christians, is surely not of this optional character. When we study it, we do not find ourselves just picking out the bits that suit us; we sense ourselves being challenged to adopt a new and distinctive criterion for our moral behavior. We have to ask, Was Jesus merely seeking to add to the stock of improving wisdom which he had inherited, or did he propound something new and different that would carry an authority, at least for his followers, of a different kind?

To this the answer must be that he did not give his teaching in a vacuum. His injunctions are not such as can be detached from the narrative of the gospels and placed alongside those of other teachers for his hearers or readers to take their choice. He gave his teaching in the context of proclaiming a state of affairs, expected in the future but already partially present, which would be sufficiently different from what we experience now to demand a different set of moral standards. This state of affairs, which he called the Kingdom of God, accords with the deepest desires and aspirations of human beings, and will assuredly be brought into actuality by the beneficent will of our Creator; but in the meantime we can find ourselves already in harmony with it, and strengthened and inspired by its dawning, if we fashion our conduct so as to live *as if* this state of affairs were already present.

When Albert Schweitzer described Jesus' teaching as an "interim ethic," he was found to be wrong insofar as he meant by this that Jesus expected an early radical change in the human environment — the coming of the Kingdom — and therefore gave teaching that was appropriate only to people who believed they were living in a short "interim" period that required no long-term calculation of consequences. But he was right in that Jesus' teaching does imply a radical nonacceptance of the present as a permanent state of affairs. God intends something for us other than the present morally dismal state of the world. By acting according to Jesus' teaching, we do not merely adopt an exceptionally demanding standard; we actually hasten the coming into being of God's "Kingdom." And if indeed we believe that this "Kingdom," as he describes it (though only in parables or images: it is not such as to be precisely defined), is an intelligible way of speaking about the destiny of a world created by God, and if we accept the challenge to fashion our lives in anticipation of it, then it is reasonable to claim that the New Testament, appropriately interpreted, provides us with authoritative guidance as we seek to make our moral choices in a world that is still far from that intended by its Creator.

CHAPTER 5

Questing for Jesus

———∞∞∞———

F or Christians, as indeed for most other readers, the heart of the New
Testament is a single person: Jesus. We have explored the sense or
senses in which Jesus may be called authoritative as a teacher. That is to say,
we have considered how a special status may be claimed for Christian Scriptures by the fact that they record what Jesus *said*. But at least as important,
if not more so, for Christian believers and for those many others who have
been attracted by him, is the question who or what he *was*.

Jesus — What Was He?

There are in fact two rather different questions here. In one sense, *what* Jesus was (and, for believers, is) is a question which has preoccupied the
church throughout its history and spawned a wide range of answers — Son
of God, God Incarnate, Second Person of the Trinity, Redeemer, Savior,
and many more. In some cases these are based on titles or descriptions
found in the New Testament; but all have acquired their present meaning
as a result of long reflection and debate and are formulated in the light of
creeds and confessional statements that owe as much to philosophy and
dogmatic theology as to Scripture. One result of this preoccupation with
what might be called the religious, or sometimes the metaphysical, signifi-

cance of Jesus has been a notable neglect of a second question about him, namely, what *kind* of person he was in his human existence. As a moral teacher and inspiration for devotion, he rapidly began to be clothed in virtues and qualities which owed more to an existing ideal of moral excellence than to any specific record of his activities; while his significance for faith and devotion very soon began to be conceived according to patterns of thought far removed from the culture from which he emerged.

It is true that the gospel accounts of his passion and crucifixion captured the medieval imagination and became the theme of intense devotion and artistic representation; but this again was narrowly focused on a few bare details of the gospel narrative and betrayed a preoccupation with the suffering that Jesus must have endured that is quite strange to the way the facts are told or even obliquely referred to in the New Testament. The familiar words, "he was despised and rejected of men," which for many people best describe what happened to Jesus, come from a prophecy of Isaiah, not from the New Testament. Serious attempts to portray the kind of man that Jesus must have been, based on such information as is offered in the gospels, began to be made only with the growth of historical criticism in the eighteenth and nineteenth centuries. It is these attempts which we have to consider when we turn to the question whether the New Testament can be regarded as reliable and authoritative when it puts before us the materials for constructing what today's readers expect of such a document: a "life" or "biography" sufficiently detailed to enable the reader to form a judgment about the character of the one whom believers claim to be Son of God and Savior of the world.

From the outset, it is important not to simplify. The question must not be phrased as if the gospels offer us unadorned facts about Jesus which the church has woven subsequently into a complex tissue of dogmatic statements and metaphysical speculation. From the earliest days of critical study it has been realized that the process of interpretation began well before the gospel records were completed, and the attempt to set apart what may be regarded as objective historical fact from the layers of religious elaboration beneath which it is buried has been a task to which generations of scholars have devoted their efforts but in which none has achieved lasting success. The "Jesus of history," it is said, is an entity quite distinct from the "Christ of faith": the second is the concern of dogmatic theologians as much as of New Testament interpreters; only the first is a proper subject of historical research, the results of which need to be assessed by criteria appropriate to that discipline. Only if this research can be shown to result in a plausible historical profile are we entitled to say that the gospels deserve our respect as reliable and authoritative accounts of the life, death and alleged resurrection of Jesus.

When we look at some of the results of this research, and the use that has been made of them, serious doubts must be awakened as to the reliability of these foundation documents of the Christian religion. The number of characterizations that have emerged from reputable scholarly research is daunting. According to some, Jesus was a dreamy Galilean romantic preaching a message of universal peace and brotherhood. According to others, he was a figure altogether alien to our culture, announcing an imminent cataclysm that would sweep away the world as we know it and inaugurate the Kingdom of God. By some he is presented in sociological terms as a "peasant," an "artisan," a "marginal Jew," a "wandering Cynic preacher," a social reformer, a liberator from the tyranny of foreign occupation and economic oppression. For others he can be located in a known religious tradition: he was one of those Jewish holy men, or *hasidim,* who were remembered for their charismatic gifts of healing and prophecy; alternatively, he was a teacher of conventional, if sometimes subversive, "wisdom," which was subsequently overlaid by the apocalyptic expectations of a church caught up in the turmoil of the Jewish revolt in the sixties of the first century. All these different profiles, and more, have been presented as the result of serious historical research; but alongside them have arisen more popular presentations, less critically based on exact study but drawing inspiration from the same gospel texts. In some of these, Jesus has appeared the model pacifist, the inspiration for nonviolent resistance to an oppressive regime. In others, he has seemed the inspirational social reformer, offering a radical scheme for justice and equality in political and social structures. In others again — and this has been a major current in church history — he has been portrayed as a stern challenger to repentance and a new life of righteousness; and to countless believers in both the evangelical and catholic traditions he has been known as a personal friend, guide, and comforter. Given this truly astonishing spectrum of characterizations, all allegedly derived from the same evidence, how can we continue to maintain that the gospels in particular, and the New Testament in general, deserve respect as an authoritative basis for a world religion?

Yet beneath this wide range of approaches there is at least a stratum of agreement. Few would now deny (though it has occasionally been denied in the past) that Jesus certainly existed; that he was crucified is a historical fact as well certified as any from antiquity; that he characteristically taught by means of parables and pithy aphorisms is the consistent testimony of three of the four gospels; that he startled his contemporaries by keeping company with those regarded as disreputable at the same time as presenting himself as a religious teacher with high moral standards is testified by both his own followers and his Jewish detractors; that he created a symbolic group of twelve followers or "apostles" to carry on his work, representing in a new form the historic twelve tribes of Israel, can hardly be fictional; and some form of confrontation with the Jewish authorities seems certain to have taken place in the temple precincts shortly before the final arrest and execution. From this slender base of historical data it may be possible to draw some further inferences; yet the variety of possible profiles — from gentle, loving, and compassionate to stern, exacting, and judgmental — remains a daunting obstacle in the way of accepting the authority of the gospels as a sure guide to the character of the religion's founder.

It is true that all this apparently conflicting evidence can be used to argue that the "real" Jesus is now irrecoverable: the eyewitnesses of the gospel story were confused and unreliable, the chroniclers were selective and biased, the narrative so replete with allegedly supernatural happenings that it must lose any claim to general credibility. But it has to be said that this is not how it has been received by its readers down the centuries, even those least disposed to accept explicitly Christian interpretations of it. Christianity, certainly, has been rejected by many of them; but few of them have regarded the story of Jesus as worthless fabrication or utterly incompetent chronicling. On the contrary, the person of Jesus has consistently exercised a fascination for believers and nonbelievers alike which is hardly explicable unless what they read in the gospels has some basis in historical truth. The only fictional figures of the past that exercise a comparable hold over the imagination, at least of Western readers, are those such as King Lear and Mephistopheles, the creations of great writers of fiction and drama. But one thing that can be said with virtual certainty about the evangelists is that the original story that they tell in their various ways was not a literary creation. It came to them, not as a whole, but in fragmentary traditions which it was their task to piece together and mold into a consecutive narrative. It is this story, and the character of the man at the center of it, which has exercised fascination over the minds of countless people whether or not they were disposed to accept the religious significance which has been placed upon it by ecclesiastical authority. Such a story, if it did not spring from the mind of a literary genius (as is clearly not the case here), must have been rooted to some degree in fact, and have been remembered and recorded with some degree of faithfulness.

The Quest for a Category

It seems, then, that in the gospels we are confronted with a character who can be dismissed neither as the fabrication of a writer nor as the product of such poor reporting that nothing significant can be made of it. However different the subsequent portraits that have emerged, the reality and basic credibility of the sitter have made a unique impression on the world. And it may be that there is a clue to the fascination it has exercised in the very variety of interpretations to which it has been exposed. Much of the effort of New Testament scholars over the last half-century has been guided by a sociological quest. Given our increasing knowledge of the religion, the culture, and the social conditions of Jesus' contemporaries, and given that his message and activities would have been unintelligible had he appeared totally alien and exotic, where can we place him within the known categories offered by his historical context? As we have seen, a great variety of templates have been tested against the evidence; but in each case there has proved to be a mismatch. Jesus was a prophet, certainly; yet (as Jesus said of John the Baptist) he was "more than a prophet." He was a teacher; yet his relationship with his students or followers was not like that of other learned Jewish teachers. His message had an urgency that seems to have been strengthened by apocalyptic language; yet (unlike other apocalyptic seers) he had much to say about moral conduct that assumed a continuation of the present world order. His lifestyle resembled that of a pagan Cynic preacher; yet his terms of reference were patently Jewish. He rarely, if ever, incurred a criminal charge through transgressing the law; yet his teaching was sharply critical of aspects of its interpretation and was frequently challenged by lawyers. His activity was such as to provoke a political response and resulted in his condemnation and death; but the charges against him, and the degree to which they were justified, remain a matter of controversy: they cannot be clearly categorized as having to do only with religion (as blasphemy) or politics (as insurrection). In short, each attempt to place him in a known religious or sociological category — prophet, reformer, charismatic, subversive, revolutionary, apocalyptist, Cynic, peasant, spiritual guide, political agitator — has added something to the portrait but failed to complete it. He stubbornly refuses to conform to any known set of characteristics; he escapes every category proposed for him.

Two words are often used to describe a person who appears, for one reason or another, to be exceptional. One is "unique"; the other is "genius." Does either of these help us to describe Jesus? The word "unique" is of course a treacherous one: what seems unique today may turn out tomorrow to have a twin or a parallel. Indeed, this has been the experience of those who have used the term in New Testament studies. Under the impact of the kind of historical criticism which sought to demonstrate that much of what Jesus did or said could be accounted for as a projection on to him of existing beliefs, customs, and practices, a criterion came into use by which it was claimed that any given element in the Jesus tradition which was unparalleled in his culture could be regarded as authentic. But this was found to have two drawbacks. For one thing, it was vulnerable to further discoveries: after more research, or with new documents being discovered, what seemed unparalleled at one moment might be found to have some parallel the next. But, secondly, it was an unsatisfactory procedure for understanding Jesus; for it amounted to assembling a list of altogether exceptional characteristics — and no human being could consist entirely of the exceptional. If Jesus was truly "unique," this uniqueness must have resulted from unique characteristics blended with other more nearly normal abilities and traits of character. But since the method excluded these from consideration, on the grounds that they were known features of his culture and might have been attributed to him by later tradition, it was found impossible by these means to build up a credible portrait of Jesus at all. In other words, if we want to say that Jesus was unique, we have to be able to say that his particular combination of unique and normal human characteristics was unparalleled, not only among his contemporaries, but among human beings in general — something which it would be quite impossible for us to know for certain. As a general term to account for the continuing fascination aroused by Jesus, the word "unique" is too risky to handle.

The word "genius," too, has its problems. It is currently used of a person who has a talent or ability which is not unusual in itself but which is developed in this case to an exceptional degree. To the statement that a person is a genius, it is appropriate to respond by asking, "A genius in what?" It is hardly possible to be an all-round genius; it is the unusual brilliance and originality displayed in the development or perfection of particular gifts or skills — artistic, literary, scientific, political — that evokes the description "genius." But again, this raises problems with respect to Jesus. What particular gifts, talents, or abilities should we say that Jesus developed to an exceptional degree? We can describe him, certainly, as a remarkable storyteller: his parables have established themselves as outstanding examples of a known Jewish genre. We can say similar things about his moral teaching, his concern for the spiritual health of individuals, his ability to discern the signs of the times, and his apparent intimacy with the God whom he called his Father. But to single out any of these as displaying "genius" seems to fail to do justice to the total impression he makes as an exceptional and memorable human being. It is precisely his combination of qualities, abilities, and disturbingly challenging attitudes which has to be reckoned with. The word "genius" seems to narrow the focus inappropriately.

Perhaps, then, we have to be content with saying that Jesus was evidently an exceptional person by the standards of his own or any other time, even though precisely how he was exceptional is a question to which the answer remains tantalizingly elusive — which indeed is part of the fascination he has exercised on countless readers of the gospels. Part of the difficulty, of course, is that it is not a question which the gospel writers were trying to answer themselves. Even in their accounts of virtually unprecedented achievements of Jesus — restoring a dead person to life or giving sight to a man born blind — they are notably restrained in their presentation and seldom emphasize their exceptionally miraculous character. Instead, these events are recounted less for their own sake than to support the claim that Jesus was (as they chose to describe him) Messiah or Son of God, with power to forgive sins and lead believers to salvation. It is on the validity of this claim that their authority as reliable sources for Christian believers must stand or fall.

Which Gospel?

The claim is succinctly formulated at the end of John's gospel, where the purpose of writing it is said to have been "that you should believe [or "come to believe"] that Jesus is the Christ, the Son of God" (20.31). But before considering whether this claim is justified we have to come to terms with a factor of which readers were totally unaware during the long centuries when every part of Scripture was regarded as equally authoritative, but which began to emerge in a troubling way when, under the influence of modern critical study, some gospels, or parts of gospels, began to be seen as containing earlier and more authentic tradition about Jeus and so as more reliable than others.

This process was made the more apparent by the rise of so-called Redaction Criticism, which is primarily a tool for explaining the remarkable relationship between the three synoptic gospels — which in some places run almost exactly parallel, in others diverge in detail, add new material, or introduce omissions or rearrangements. A close comparison of equivalent sections of narrative has been found to reveal characteristic tendencies and interests in each of the gospels which may be assigned to the particular purpose of each of the gospel writers. By the use of this tool it has been possible to establish (or at least argue for) a distinct profile of each evangelist. In the previous era of "form criticism" the evangelists were portrayed as mere editors, coping as best they could with the disordered and fragmentary material relating to Jesus which they received from the traditions already current in the church. But the new critical technique revealed them as active thinkers — scholars even began to call them (like themselves) "theologians" —

deliberately arranging and fashioning the sayings and narratives in such a way as to reveal their significance for their readers. Studies of the gospels consequently became less centered on Jesus and more on the individual writer, and the reader came away with a sense of having gained a vivid acquaintance with Mark, Matthew, or Luke as writers and thinkers — though at the expense, it seemed, of any advance in knowledge of the person of Jesus himself. For example, Luke's portrait of Jesus, with its emphasis on a more universal mission and a more comprehensive view of humanity (giving a larger place to women, for instance) seemed to come alive in a new way and to be in contrast with Matthew's, where the focus is more on relationship with the Jewish law and the correct transmission of the teaching. But which Jesus was authentic; which should we follow? In other words, the question with which we began, whether the gospels give us an account which validates the claims made for Jesus, has to be rephrased: Does Matthew, or Mark, or Luke, give us such an account?

But the moment this question is asked, the whole inquiry takes a different turn. It is true that in many respects these different accounts of Jesus are compatible with each other and may even be said to complement each other. Indeed, the idea of a "harmony" of all the gospels, creating a single narrative out of the four, is as old as the second century and was still being made use of when critical analysis got under way in the nineteenth century. But the moment it is recognized that the gospels do *not* always say the same thing, and that we may find in them accounts of the teaching and ministry of Jesus that allow different conclusions to be drawn; the moment it is accepted (as has been the case now for a century or more among New Testament scholars) that one version of a saying or of an event in the life of Jesus may be more authentic and nearer the historical truth than another; the moment we begin to identify and question the original contribution, or "theology," of each evangelist — then we have to ask on which of these accounts we are to base our understanding of the significance of Jesus. The claim of "Holy Scripture" is that it is the channel by which the revelation of divinely authorized truth is made available to human beings. But once we find ourselves asking which part of Scripture or which scriptural writer we may best trust to convey this revelation, we are inevitably questioning their scriptural authority. We are treating them as we might treat other sources of historical knowledge, comparing them with each other for reliability and even, in some cases perhaps, being ready to discard a portion of them as relatively unimportant or even misleading.

In one sense this is what Christians have been doing since very early times. In the second century Marcion proposed the radical expedient of excluding the Old Testament altogether and allowing only one of the Gospels (Luke) and ten of Paul's letters to remain in the New. Until the end of the third there was doubt whether Revelation should be included in Holy Scripture. And, as is well known, even such an impassioned advocate of the power of Scripture to move hearts and minds as Martin Luther could dismiss the Letter of James as worthless for salvation, despite its assured place in the New Testament canon. And, to a lesser degree, most Christians have followed his example, in that they regard some portions of the Bible as of high value and importance, while others may be passed over altogether. These preferences have resulted in significantly different forms of the Christian faith. Those who found in Paul's Letter to the Romans the most powerful expression of the human condition in relation to God's justice and mercy were those who fashioned a theology that laid great emphasis on the crucial importance of faith and the gracious acceptance by God of those who acknowledge their sinfulness. Those (and there have been many also) who found in John's gospel the quintessence of the Christian message were seized above all by its portrayal of an infinitely loving God and have laid less emphasis (as John's gospel does) on forgiveness and grace.

A "Holy Book" for Christianity?

This selectivity, which consciously or unconsciously has been exercised by Christian readers at least since the Reformation, raises a question that has a bearing on our attempt to establish Jesus' character and intentions. Was the religion he founded ever intended to have its own "Holy Scripture"? Christianity, in its earliest form, was understood as demanding that no place on earth should be uniquely "holy"; that (unlike Judaism) no race or polity should be uniquely privileged; that (unlike Islam) no specific language was mandatory for worship or study. It is true that with the passage of time these austere demands were modified under the pressure of universal religious instincts: holy places were established, certain forms of church order, and sometimes of civic life, came to be regarded as divinely authorized, and even certain vernacular translations of the Scriptures, such as the King James Version, came to be regarded as having inherited something of the inspiration of the original. But was the Christian religion ever intended to follow the example of others and have its own "holy book"? The available writings, after all, did not make any claim to divine authorization such as that implied in Moses' commission to hand down God's law, or Muhammad's experience of receiving revelation at the direct dictation of God. They were confessedly the work of men (later regarded, with little historical justification, as apostles or "apostolic") who wrote to fill particular needs in the life of the early church, or even in some cases (as is now increasingly accepted) to amplify or even correct what others had already written. Out of this disparate and occasional material the church, within a century or two, had fashioned a collection of books which could neither be altered nor added to and which came to be accepted as the unalterable canon of "Holy Scripture." Was this development in accord with the mind of the religion's founder?

Any answer to this question is bound to be speculative. Jesus must certainly have regarded the Hebrew Scriptures as inspired, as conveying the word of God, and as essential to the life and religion of his contemporaries. Much of his teaching was in relation to it, and though his interpretation of it was frequently innovative, he gave no hint of wishing that it should be superseded, or indeed that anyone should seriously contemplate living without it. On the other hand, he appears to have made no provision for a written record of his own teaching. It is true that his ministry seems to have been quite narrowly focused on his own people, for whom he could hardly have imagined a radical change in religious observance; yet there is also a strain of universalism in his recorded words, and occasionally in his actions, such that it is reasonable to think that he sensed at least the possibility of his "gospel" being preached far outside the confines of the Jewish world. In that case, what would be the resources available to these non-Jewish Christians for their instruction and guidance? On one — now rather dated — view of his self-understanding, the question might not have arisen at all. If he genuinely expected the Kingdom, understood as a radically new state of affairs, to come within his own or his followers' lifetime, then no "scriptures" would be necessary anyway: the prophecy of Jeremiah would have come true, that God would write his law directly on people's hearts, with no other mediation necessary between him and his human creatures. But even on the more generally accepted view, that Jesus envisaged an interval before any radical change took place long enough for his teaching to be heard and responded to over a period of time, there is no evidence that he gave thought to the preservation of his words and the recording of the crucial episodes of his life. On the other hand, we have no grounds for saying that he would have been opposed to the creation of Christian "holy books" along with (but not superseding) the Torah, or that his followers would be unfaithful to him if they began to compose such books and if in due course they gave them a standard and unalterable form as part of the "canon" of Holy Scripture. We can say with some confidence that Jesus was a child of his time and his culture: he accepted without question the sanctity of the written record of God's self-revelation to his people. But what we cannot say is that the emergence of the New Testament, and its eventual canonical status as a "holy book," was either in accordance with or contrary to his intentions.

The Category of Messiah

This conclusion (such as it is) is of importance in our quest for the legitimacy and authority of the Christian Scriptures. But it is also significant in relation to the question with which we began this chapter, namely, the closer definition of the person of Jesus. There can be no doubt that he was in at least this respect a typical member of his race and nation: he was reverential toward the Hebrew Scriptures and undoubtedly regarded them as "Holy." But is this compatible with the claims made for him? It is sometimes thought that one who was genuinely the expected Messiah would, in his person, supersede the religious traditions and scriptures that had gone before. The Samaritan woman is reported as having said, quite correctly according to some Jewish beliefs, "When the Messiah comes, he will make everything clear to us" (John 4.25). But this was not to say that we can then stop reading the Bible; only that in the new age its meaning will become un-ambiguously clear. And this is precisely what Jesus is reported to have been doing. His comments on a series of biblical commandments in the Sermon on the Mount, though they are sometimes taken as a rewriting of the laws of Moses, are equally capable of being taken (as I believe they should be) as reinterpretations in the spirit of (but more radical than) the rabbinic prin-ciple of "a fence round the law": killing is always wrong, and anger can lead to homicide, so avoid anger as if it were equally criminal! His exposition was fully in accord with the expectation of a Messiah who would "make ev-erything clear." Whether, in truth, he *was* that Messiah, and whether in-deed the Messiah-category is helpful at all to us now, are questions which cannot be answered from Scripture alone. But that Jesus both fulfilled and at the same time refined and re-interpreted his people's expectation of a Messiah is a reasonably assured conclusion from the gospel evidence, and was affirmed from very early times by his followers when they began calling him — possibly in his lifetime, certainly after the resurrection — not just Jesus, but the Messiah, the Christ.

But this raises a question that has to be faced. What purchase on our minds can this expectation of a "messiah" have in the twenty-first century? Two millennia have passed since it expressed a lively hope in the minds of Jesus' contemporaries. Since then there have been movements in both Juda-ism and Christianity which have revived an enthusiastic expectation of an imminent deliverance, and there are still fringe Christian groups today which see the threats that menace humanity as signs of an approaching Ar-mageddon that will prepare for a messianic "coming." But the great major-ity of the world's population, whether of Christian, Jewish, or other faiths, have long ceased to let their lives be influenced by any serious conviction that the near future will see a radical change brought about by a divinely commissioned reformer such as could fit the designation "Messiah." And since the Christian and (to a lesser extent) the Jewish Scriptures so often and so insistently affirm that such a "coming" is imminent, must they not lose their authority, and with it their claim to "holiness," when we finally admit that we no longer believe anything of the sort?

It is important, first, to clarify how this messianic dimension of the Jewish faith arose and what it signified. Anthropologists like to compare it with the cargo cults of primitive peoples, who daily expected a supernatural ship from the sea to bring them liberation from their oppressors; and historians might agree that the history of the Jewish people since Hellenistic times had been a comparable one of colonial oppression, making it natural for the belief to arise that God would send a liberator to inaugurate a new era of freedom and prosperity. This was indeed the period when messianic expectations flourished to an exceptional degree (though the evidence does not allow us to be sure how widely they were shared throughout the population); and we might conclude that the whole concept of Messiah was the result of such circumstances, was developed among people of a crudely simplistic turn of mind, and can therefore be relegated to a relatively primitive stage of religious development.

But this analysis is too simple: it ignores the very deep roots of messianism, which can be traced right through the Hebrew Scriptures. A summary account of these convictions might run as follows. God created the world and saw that it was good. But look around at the world as it is, and evil is rampant. There is injustice, there is want, there is oppression; and in the New Testament period there was the further scandal of a foreign regime occupying the land of God's chosen people. Clearly, then, the creation was not, or not yet, as its creator intended it to be. But God is not powerless. If he intended it otherwise, his intention must surely take effect: a new age must be in the divine project, and human beings are to live in expectation of its coming. But how would it come into being? Here opinions were divided. Some thought in terms of a miraculous change of heart occurring by a kind of divine pressure among God's own chosen people and radiating from them to the rest of humanity. But others, perhaps the majority, saw the need for a human figure, exceptionally endowed with the resources and influence required to bring about the change — a Messiah. A simplistic version of this was a supernaturally endowed military leader who would throw out the alien colonists and institute a new period of independence for the Jewish people, who might then live a truly God-fearing life and extend their influence to others. More sophisticated scenarios could be distilled from Old Testament prophecy that laid greater emphasis on the moral character of the deliverer and his absolute commitment to justice and peace. But the heart of the matter was the conviction that the present state of affairs could not be according to God's purpose when he created the world: the future must hold the realization or consummation of his design. And if it made sense to think that an individual person, exceptionally endowed with the Holy Spirit, might bring in this new era, then one might even say that the appearance of such a person was part of the original project of creation. As an ancient rabbinic text puts it, one of the things already present at the very moment of creation was "the name of the Messiah."

Stated in these terms, faith in a messianic age (whether or not brought about by an individual Messiah) is by no means something that can be dismissed as an outdated phenomenon. It is a necessary consequence of the fundamental religious perception that God created the world, not capriciously or without responsibility for its future, but seriously and with a discernible moral purpose. And there is a further corollary which follows from the creation of free human beings to inhabit this world, a corollary that is taken seriously by all three Abrahamic faiths, namely, that these human beings bear some responsibility for the world in which they find themselves, and that the quality of the stewardship they perform — their reverence, their justice, their compassion, and now their responsibility for the environment in which they find themselves — will be a crucial factor affecting the time and the manner in which God will establish the new era.

If this was the basic framework for religious belief and religious hopes in the time of Christ, then all the evidence points to Jesus having engaged with it and given it a relevance and urgency which is still powerfully significant today. Of course the messianic idea was capable of being interpreted in crude and nationalistic forms, and it appears (though the evidence is somewhat ambiguous) that it was exploited by a number of spurious claimants in the decades immediately before and after Christ. But for the serious religious mind the important reality was, not the Messiah himself, but the age he would inaugurate. It has seldom been the case that a genuinely religious person "claimed" to be Messiah: it was rather that signs were discerned of a new age dawning and some exceptional person was recognized and acknowledged as the agent who was bringing it about, the "Messiah." But this implied that minds would be trained and ready to recognize the real thing when it came — not a nationalistic movement spuriously claiming worldwide significance, but a moral transformation in individuals and in society that would herald a truly new era of human flourishing. It is into this scheme that the teaching of Jesus about the Kingdom — a state of affairs which is already vestigially present in acts of love, generosity, and self-sacrifice, but which still awaits its full realization in the future — and the training he gave to his followers to be alert to its dawning, most naturally fit. And insofar as the gospels are a record of teaching delivered to that end, and the New Testament as a whole a record of the church being schooled to cherish and promote the moral and religious preparation required for its realization, this record — these Scriptures — acquires authority as the indispensable channel of information and inspiration for those who accept the hope and the vision of God's ultimate purpose for the world and its inhabitants.

The Time Scale

But even if we accept this messianic context as giving both intelligibility and relevance to the gospel message, we still have to come to terms with an awkward and apparently unassimilable feature of it. We have been speaking as if the messianic idea, and the sense of the necessary fruition of God's purposes in a new age, had a timeless relevance, regardless of any particular moment in history or in cultural and religious development. But the teaching of Jesus, though much of it has a timeless quality and speaks of the Kingdom as a reality which may be perceived at any time and in any place, nevertheless is at times disturbingly time-specific. "There are some standing here who shall not see death until they have seen the Kingdom of God come in power" (Mark 9.1). It would be a crass misreading of the gospels — even that of John, though in this case the problem is less acute — if one were to extract from them a sequence of timeless truths and injunctions and ignore the urgency with which Jesus demands action *while there is still time*. Something decisive, a radical change in the human condition, he seems to say, is about to occur, not in the unspecified future, but within his own generation — and must we not say that he was wrong, that it did not do so? And does this not mean that his authority is thereby weakened? And do not the gospels thereby forfeit our trust as holy writings designed to lead us on a path that leads to the truth about God and his relationship to human beings?

The key, I believe, to answering this question is a title that was certainly given to Jesus in his lifetime and was indeed the one that came most naturally to his contemporaries when they sought to sum up the impact he made. "They held him to be a prophet" is Matthew's report of the crowd whose assumed support of Jesus made the authorities afraid to act against him (21.46); he was "a prophet mighty in word and deed" is how some disciples described him immediately after the crucifixion (Luke 24.19); and Jesus seems to have acknowledged the role when he quoted in reference to himself the maxim that "a prophet is not without honor save in his own country" (Mark 6.4). His message, therefore, was clearly perceived to be in the prophetic idiom, as this was understood in a culture shaped by the Old Testament prophets; and this idiom had the same combination of time-specific urgency and openness to postponement that troubles us in the case of Jesus. When the prophets pleaded for a change of heart in the face of an impending national disaster, they inevitably (and in the circumstances doubtless correctly) counseled immediate response, given that delay could precipitate and even aggravate the calamity. But if in fact things turned out otherwise, if the crisis seemed averted or at least delayed, the prophet did not lose credibility; on the contrary, his message was subsequently reinterpreted as a warning applicable to a similar train of events that might occur sometime in the future. The prophet's task was to "read the signs of the times"; but this would have had little impact if it had seemed that he was warning only of consequences far in the future; it was therefore necessary for him to use language that demanded an urgent response. But as time passed, and if the crisis either did not materialize or turned out to be less serious than the prophet had warned, the prophecy lost none of its seriousness. Indeed, its summons to be alert to the gravity of such a situation and its warning of the consequences of inertia in the face of it might be even more relevant at some time in the future. The very essence of the call to action lay in its urgency. In the event, the crisis might turn out differently; but this did not rob the prophecy of its validity. The message might be no less relevant later on.

We may apply the same analysis to the apparently unfulfilled predictions of Jesus. "Repent, for the Kingdom of heaven is at hand" is the manifesto placed at the head of his teaching by two of the evangelists. This distinguishes Jesus at once from other moral teachers of his time and culture, who spelled out their counsel in maxims and examples of timeless application: they took it for granted that lessons from past experience would continue to provide the best guidance for conduct in any conceivable future. But Jesus spoke of imminent change, and of a new style of moral conduct that was appropriate to such a moment in history. The urgency of his message was such as to evoke immediate response. Had he phrased it in terms of developments at some unspecified time in the future, it could have had no comparable impact on his hearers' lives and characters. But equally, as a prophetic summons, its validity did not depend on its complete realization within the expected time scale.

In the event, his predictions were at least partially fulfilled. Within the lifetime of many of his hearers Jerusalem was virtually destroyed and a new, life-changing religion had taken root in many parts of the Roman Empire. This might not amount to all that was understood by "the Kingdom." Jesus had given rise to expectations of more radical change, and after his death his followers continued to look forward to a "coming" that would be of a different order altogether. But it was more than enough to give credibility to the thrust of his teaching, which was that circumstances are such — will always be such — that alert attention and immediate response are demanded of any who seek to live according to the will of God and to promote the values of the Kingdom. As a stimulus to inspire an enhanced morality, Jesus' prophetic time scale was exactly right: not so catastrophically imminent as to induce moral paralysis, but not far enough away to permit putting off decision and action. "The Kingdom of heaven is upon you — within this generation!" The moment for response is — and always will be — *now*.

Since then, two thousand years have passed. Can a message and a challenge so discredited by its implausible time frame be of relevance now? Before dismissing it on these grounds, we need to be clear about exactly what the prophecies amounted to and to what extent they were either unfulfilled or unrelated to a specific moment in time. It is often imagined that when speaking of the coming Kingdom Jesus was aligning himself with those apocalyptic writers who envisaged a scenario of cosmic cataclysms leading to the creation of "a new heaven and a new earth." The most familiar of these is that which we read in the Revelation of St. John. We may assume that it was inspired at least in part by the prophetic strand in Jesus' teaching, which made it seem plausible that those who were already suffering for their new faith would be rewarded by the establishment of a new dispensation such that their persecutors would receive their just deserts and the saints of God be finally allotted their place of honor. On any literal reading of such predictions, it can only be said that none of this has taken place, and it would be naive to suppose that it will do so in the near future. If, on the other hand, they are read with allowance for the poetic elaboration inherent in the apocalyptic idiom, they may be found to be doing no more than exploiting the same convention as we have seen in Old Testament prophecy, making predictions of what is likely to happen in the very near future — predictions which must therefore be taken with full seriousness. Such predictions do not lose their credibility if they turn out to be, not so much accurate forecasts of impending events as depictions of historical sequences that are liable to occur in the future and which challenge human beings to respond with a radically different set of moral priorities. It is true that the apocalyptic writers of the Hellenistic and Roman periods of Jewish history were so outraged by the catastrophe (as they saw it) of the destruction of their national and religious heritage that they came to believe passionately in the inevitability of a God of justice soon intervening to vindicate his faithful servants and humiliate their enemies. Yet they were careful to formulate their predictions in coded form, not just to avoid such explicit political statements as might incur the danger of immediate suppression and persecution, but to leave open the possibility of fulfillment in other ways and at other times. What they forecast as certain, in a world ultimately subject to the moral and religious values of its Creator, were the inevitable consequences of idolatry, injustice, and unrestrained political ambition. Precisely when the moment of retribution would come to pass was a less important matter — though it was always necessary to be prepared for it, and those who were suffering now needed to be assured that their ultimate justification would not be indefinitely delayed.

In Mark 13, and in the corresponding chapters of Matthew and Luke, Jesus is represented as speaking in the same idiom — so much so that this chapter is generally called "the little apocalypse." The discourse is triggered by his prophecy of the destruction of the Jerusalem temple, a catastrophe which did indeed take place in the lifetime of Jesus' hearers. It goes on to predict trials and afflictions which would befall Jesus' followers, and these, too, duly came to pass. It then moves into a more explicitly "apocalyptic" mode, describing the moment when the Son of man would be "coming in the clouds with power and great glory." It is likely to have been a prediction of this kind which caused the first generation of Christians to expect an early *parousia* — a "second coming" of Christ that would bring in a new age of justice and vindication of the righteous. To this extent, we may certainly say that Jesus must have raised false expectations or at least laid himself open to misunderstanding. But we must also recognize that the fault may have lain with the disciples. What we have described as the prophetic or apocalyptic idiom was essentially ambiguous and open-ended. Part of what was predicted duly came to pass; part of it remained unfulfilled but could be understood as a scenario that would inevitably occur in God's own time in the future. And the scenario itself, though some certainly took it literally for a while, could have been intended in more general terms as an imaginative description of the kind of moral regeneration which lay at the heart of mature messianic expectations and which must surely lie within the ultimate purposes of the Creator.

One of those who evidently did take these predictions literally, but then came to understand them as indicating a less immediate dénouement, was St. Paul. In his letters he has left us a personal record of the way his understanding changed. It is to his contribution to the New Testament that we must now turn.

CHAPTER 6

Reckoning with Paul

F or most of the church's history the study of Paul took the form of using
any texts which come down to us under his name to build up a more or
less systematic account of his beliefs (his "theology"). In this scheme, it was
of little consequence from which letter any piece of evidence came, or even
in what context; the simple fact of occurring within the received corpus of
Paul's New Testament writings was sufficient to give it authority and justify
its place in the resulting system. Any word, verse, or paragraph, since it oc-
curred in "Holy Scripture," must be assumed "inspired," authoritative, and
true. The task was to bring it all together into a coherent and intelligible
whole.

The more recent critical approach to the New Testament has altered
the task beyond recognition. It is not just that some of the thirteen letters
which bear his name have come to be regarded as more likely to have been
written by one or more of his followers and are therefore no longer used as
direct evidence for his thought. A more fundamental change has come
about through the recognition that even the certainly authentic letters cannot be relied on to give consistent evidence of a settled deposit of belief.
These letters were written in response to different recipients in various circumstances, and may be expected to reveal a difference of emphasis and approach; they cover a period of some twelve to fifteen years in Paul's life, long
enough for his thought to have evolved and developed; and in places he may

be quoting from a tradition which existed before his time, commenting upon it, and possibly modifying it to adapt to new circumstances. To construct a consistent "theology" out of such materials is bound to be a complex task. Some scholars, indeed, regard it as impracticable.

A further assumption lies behind modern study which would have been altogether strange during the long centuries when every part of Scripture was regarded as equally "inspired." It is an assumption which sustains most studies of ancient history, namely, that the closer in time that a document stands to the event it records, the greater its value as evidence. For the practitioner of historical criticism, Mark's gospel tends to be given priority over the others simply on the grounds that it is likely to have been written first and is therefore better evidence than the others for "the historical Jesus." Similarly, there is especial interest in Paul's earliest letters (arguably 1 Thessalonians or Galatians) as representing the earliest written texts in the New Testament, and still more in those passages where it seems that Paul is not composing in his own style but quoting some already existing tradition or text. Since Paul nowhere refers to any written gospel, it seems safe to assume that none was yet in circulation; in that case his letters are the earliest Christian writings we possess. And if, in those letters, we can detect him using still earlier sources or documents, we feel we are getting very close indeed to the beginnings of Christianity. In 1 Corinthians 15 Paul does this explicitly: "I handed on to you the tradition I had received. . . . this is what we all proclaim, and this is what you believed" (15.3, 11). In other cases it is less clear — ancient manuscripts had no quotation marks, and we have to infer from points of vocabulary, style, or arrangement that Paul is not writing out of his own head but is reminding his readers of something they already know. The most compelling example is the so-called "Christ Hymn" in Philippians 2.5-11: it has a discernibly poetic structure (some have detected a metrical pattern in the assumed Aramaic original); it contains theological statements about Christ that are not recognizably Pauline and may well be "primitive," that is, have been in use before his time; and it is abruptly introduced into the context by the pronoun "who," in a manner which is familiar from hymns and prayers in many cultures. "Almighty God, who . . ." is still one of the commonest forms of prayer in the church today. All of this strongly suggests that Paul was quoting an existing hymn or prayer from the early days of Christian worship. Not that we can be sure that he was quoting it accurately, or even that he may not have been offering his own adapted version of it. Yet there remains a strong impression that here we are touching a very ancient seam of early Christian belief and worship, which can then be used as a template against which to measure the extent to which Paul's thought moves forward, and possibly away, from the faith which inspired the disciples very soon after the resurrection.

Paul and Jesus

But (some will ask) was his faith *ever* the same faith as that of those disciples? His references to any known fact about Jesus other than the crucifixion and the resurrection, or to any word of his teaching, are extremely sparse; and the religion which he elaborated from this small basis of fact, combined with some highly subjective spiritual experiences of his own, has been regarded by some as the real origin of Christianity as we know it today. The original Jesus of Nazareth may have borne little resemblance to the glorified Christ we encounter in Paul's letters; but it is the latter which has been a dominating influence on Christian theology ever since. Paul, according to these critics, was the inventor of Christianity; the real Jesus, who may still be discerned in the gospels despite the overlay of later theological elaboration, was in many ways doubtless exceptional and the inspirer of a rich religious and moral heritage, but entirely human and innocent of the extravagant claims made for him by those who have taken Paul as their guide.

To counter this view, which is mainly advanced by non-Christian critics anxious to liberate Jesus from the contamination (as they see it) of subsequent Christian doctrine, scholars have labored to establish continuity between Jesus and Paul and to scotch the idea that Paul was doing anything other than drawing out the implications of what had been achieved by Christ through the crucifixion and resurrection. They have on their side some explicit statements of Paul himself, who, in a rare passage of autobiography (Gal. 1.13ff.), describes how he conferred, even if only for short periods, with the Jerusalem apostles and was careful to bring his own preaching into line with theirs. And even if he seems to make little use of the information which in due course became the substance of the gospel narratives, it is reasonable to think that this may have been knowledge he already shared with his correspondents and that he had no need to rehearse it with them: his task was to explain to them what it implied for their faith and their conduct. In particular he had to devote much of his attention to the problems arising from a mixed Christian community of Jews and Gentiles, problems which nothing in the tradition about Jesus can have explicitly addressed. Unless, therefore, it can be shown that his thought was actually incompatible with the teaching and intentions of Jesus — which would be difficult to demonstrate — Paul may reasonably be given the benefit of the doubt and allowed to stand as a faithful witness to the apostolic faith.

That last phrase, however, begs a question, and one that bears directly on the theme of this book, which is the authority, and hence the "holiness," of the Christian Scriptures. It was an axiom of the early church that writings they had collected into what became known as the New Testament deserved their place in it by reason of being "apostolic." In its most obvious sense, this would have meant that each of the writings could be assigned to an author who was one of Jesus' apostles; and the primary qualification for this title, as we know from what Paul says on the subject, was that an apostle should either have been a follower of Jesus in his lifetime or a witness to his resurrection (or, in the special case of Paul himself, to the resurrected Jesus appearing at a later time). But in the case of at least two of the gospels (Mark and Luke) and of certain other books, the assumed authors certainly belonged neither to this original company of witnesses nor to the original Twelve appointed by Jesus. The term "apostolic," therefore, had to be stretched to mean something like "belonging to the apostles' generation and written by persons associated with the apostles." But it has been fairly pointed out that all this contains an element of fantasy. It was not known, even in the early centuries, who were the authors of some of the New Testament books; and critical study has made it seem extremely unlikely that all the gospels and epistles were written within the lifetime of any but the most long-lived of the original apostles (we must remember that to live beyond the age of around sixty was unusual at the time). Moreover, the criterion was by no means a safe one: gospels which later were regarded as inauthentic and were excluded from Scripture were routinely ascribed to apostles or resurrection witnesses (Thomas, Mary Magdalene, James, and others), and it was not easy to show that the credentials of the authors of the received canonical writings were much better. In practice, reliance was placed more on the respect with which the writings were regarded throughout the churches and their consistency with received doctrine than on their established pedigree as "apostolic."

On both these counts it is evident that Paul's writings passed the test. Even so selective a critic as Marcion admitted most of them to his list of acceptable Scriptures, and the church rapidly came to accept them as an essential supplement to the gospels, as consistent with the faith they had received, and so as "apostolic." It is therefore not surprising that modern attempts to drive a wedge between the religion preached by Paul and the assumed "primitive" gospel of Jesus have not been successful. It is of course true that there are profound differences of style and presentation. The gospel story and the activity of the disciples after the resurrection are set within a strictly Palestinian environment and move little outside the culture of the parent Jewish community. Paul, by contrast, takes the gospel far away from its small provincial origins and brings it into dialogue with a cosmopolitan religious and intellectual world. The claim that he "invented" Christianity can be allowed to be true in the sense that it was he who made it possible for the Jesus movement to cross the cultural and religious boundaries within which it had first flourished. But it is harder to defend if it is taken to mean that there is serious discontinuity between Paul and the earliest traditions about Jesus.

But this, of course, is not to say that what we have in Paul's letters is interchangeable with what we have in the gospels or even always consistent with it. His insistence on the gravity and universality of human sinfulness and the free and gracious gift of salvation independent of religious observances is something which can hardly be inferred directly from the recorded teaching of Jesus; indeed, for Paul it was an inference, not from anything Jesus said or did himself, but from the crucial fact (as he saw it) that the crucifixion was a demonstration of God's love for sinners, a gift to be appropriated not by religious observances, or even, apparently, by attention to Jesus' moral and religious teaching, but by self-knowledge, penitence, and faith. It was a message which the early church evidently found to be in accordance with the understanding they had reached of Jesus' death and resurrection, and to be consistent with Paul's claim to be an "apostle." His surviving letters were consequently dubbed "apostolic," and their teaching, which covered a wide range of issues confronting the church, was accepted without apparent hesitation as authoritative. Already before the end of the New Testament period these letters were called "scripture" (2 Pet. 3.16). They were quoted throughout the second century in support of individual presentations of the Christian faith, and by the beginning of the third century their place in the canon of Scripture was sufficiently assured for theologians to write commentaries upon them and attempt to bring Paul's vigorous and not always consistent or easily intelligible affirmations into an orderly and coherent system of belief.

A New Look at Paul

But even if the letters can be shown to be not inconsistent with the tradition preserved in the gospels, are they consistent among themselves? Does Paul propound a single and universally applicable exposition of the faith, or are we confronted with an all-too-human amalgam of complex emotions and religious instincts that makes any systematic analysis impossible and limits the application of his teaching to certain situations and certain types of person? In the nineteenth century this question was raised in a sharp form by the popularity of Freudian psychology. What was it that caused the revolution in Paul's attitude toward the Christian religion? We may answer, his conversion experience on the Damascus road. But when we read his own account of his spiritual development and of his struggle with a pervading sense of sin and unworthiness, do we not recognize a well-known psychological state? Was it not the agonized repression of his early years, caused by the useless attempt to make himself perfect in the eyes of the Jewish law, which finally burst out in the freedom offered him by the liberating gospel of Christ? This is not to deny that he may have had an experience such as is described three times in Acts and alluded to in Galatians 1; but it sets this experience in the context of a known psychological condition, which also helps to explain his apparent inhibitions in sexual matters and the violence of his outbursts against his former co-religionists, whom he identified with the constraints which had caused such painful repression in his younger days. Hence his enduring appeal to those whose own emotional development has been similar and whose crushing sense of sinfulness is dramatically relieved by the message of one who underwent similar torment and was granted such decisive liberation.

An analysis along these lines has inspired many studies of Paul, and has had considerable influence on popular attitudes toward him. But it implies an unwelcome consequence. The psychological condition ascribed to Paul before his conversion may be one shared by a great many people; but it is also one which a great many people do *not* experience. Does this mean that Paul's presentation of the gospel is of use only to some? Must those who have suffered from no such repression lay his letters aside as not for them (and therefore, inevitably, as something less than "Holy Scripture")? Must we all pay equal respect to writings by a person who, from a psychological point of view, might be described as seriously unbalanced?

This question, fortunately, no longer poses itself in so sharp a form. Paul's letters are one area of New Testament study where it is possible to claim that there has been positive progress, a "new look." For centuries the interpretation of Paul had been profoundly influenced by some highly subjective factors. Martin Luther had found in Paul's rejection of the "Law" an exact parallel to his own experience of the rites and (as he saw them) oppressive abuses that had grown up in the Roman Catholic Church; Calvin had been able to find a strict doctrine of predestination confirmed by a few verses in Romans 11; and Sigmund Freud's followers had found in Paul's sense of inability to fulfill the demands the Law made upon him evidence of a psychological state of repression and frustration characteristically liable to explode in the form of a "conversion." These influences contributed to a general understanding of the Jewish Law as an impossibly heavy burden, making demands that could never be strictly fulfilled, and corresponding, it seemed, to the picture obtained from Jesus' attacks on the Pharisees, who "lay intolerable burdens on people's backs and will not lift a finger to lighten them" (Luke 11.46). But this interpretation was hardly compatible either with what is otherwise known about the Pharisees or with Paul's explicit claim that, before his conversion, he was, "with regard to righteousness in the eyes of the law, impeccable" (Phil. 3.6). A better understanding of the nature of the obligations imposed by Jewish law and the sense of privilege that went with them has now made it possible to read what Paul says about it without the inheritance of either Luther's preoccupation with the legalism (as he saw it) of the Catholic tradition or the psychological repression attributed to him by Freudian psychoanalytic theory. It has been realized that there is no evidence that strictly observant Jews in his time (or indeed subsequently) found the Law an intolerable burden or an unrealizable ideal.

Moreover, the impact of sociology on biblical studies has set the whole question in a different light. Paul's problems with the Law were not a matter of one person's choices and obligations. What was at stake was one's social and religious identity as part of a defined community. To cease observing the Law — that is, keeping the observances which went with a strict interpretation of the Jewish way of life — meant separating oneself from the Jewish community or else submitting to the penalties which the synagogue could impose for transgressions. For Jews converting to Christianity, there was a great temptation not to forfeit the sense of social solidarity and personal identity which went with membership in the local Jewish community: why should one not continue as a faithful observer of traditional customs and obligations but at the same time practice the worship and accept the beliefs of this new form of Judaism that was being promoted by the church? But Paul recognized that it was impossible to place value on these observances without nullifying the new freedom obtained through Christ to live and worship in a community that was bound by none of them but only by a moral law. In order to remain an acceptable person within Jewish communities, Paul astonishingly appears to have accepted the necessity of very severe punishments executed by the synagogue (forty strokes save one administered on no fewer [he says] than five occasions, 2 Cor. 11.24). But he also made it clear that he underwent this for tactical reasons only — so as to be able to continue to influence his fellow Jews by remaining a member of their synagogues, even if it meant submitting to the punishments prescribed for what they saw as his transgressions (1 Cor. 9.20). But for the purpose of explaining to church members that they were not bound to any such observances and had an identity quite separate from, and as powerful as, that of synagogue members, he spoke to them of the Law as a servitude from which the gospel of Christ liberates all believers; and, when in their company, he conducted himself (as he says himself) as a Gentile, demonstrating by personal example the independence that all Christians now enjoyed from allegiance to any other ethnic or religious community.

Thus we may exempt Paul from the charge of being too tortured and unstable an individual to be trusted as a reliable guide to Christian belief. But there is another question which might be equally damaging to his authority. His letters — or at least those which are generally regarded as authentic — cover, as we have said, a relatively short period of around a dozen years (between 50 and 62 C.E.). But this was long enough for his thought to develop and, if need be, change — in which case we should have to ask how a writer who says different things at different times can be regarded as authoritative for those who revere his writing as part of Scripture, and how that Scripture itself can be regarded as "Holy" if it contains material so clearly influenced by changeable human factors. In short, we have to ask, Does Paul change his mind? And, if so, are these changes sufficiently important to affect our estimation of his authority?

The Destiny of the Jews and the Future of the World

As I have said, it was only recently that attention began to be paid by scholars to any such possibility. It was an article by C. H. Dodd in 1934 that first gave an impetus to such study. Starting from the general consensus that 1 Thessalonians is Paul's first extant letter, Dodd suggested that there were two questions about which Paul appears to have said something very different in later letters from what he had said in earlier ones, and that therefore, to this extent at least, Paul may be said to have changed his views. The first of these has to do with Paul's attitude to the Jewish people. Acts 17 tells the story of the opposition which Paul encountered in Thessalonica from the synagogue: he was forced to leave quite rapidly. In his first letter to the Thessalonians he alludes to the "great opposition" he has experienced himself from the Jewish authorities (2.2), and compliments the Thessalonian Christians for having remained firm in their faith despite the similar harassment they have experienced. He then goes on to accuse the Jews of having been those who "killed the Lord Jesus and the prophets, and drove us out, and are so heedless of God's will and such enemies of their fellow men that they hinder us from telling the Gentiles how they may be saved." As a result, he says, "retribution has over-taken them for good and all!" (2.16) — the expression is *eis telos,* which de-notes absolute finality. The retribution is total and irremediable. But this is not at all the language of the long section of Romans where he discusses the place of the Jewish people in the scheme of salvation, and suggests that they may not have "fallen" so much as merely "stumbled," and that it is possible to look forward to their restoration as the chosen people of God (11.11-12). Faced with this apparent incompatibility between the two statements, Dodd ab-jured the harmonizing efforts of previous scholars and turned instead to pos-sible explanations in the biography of Paul — perhaps the change was the re-sult of maturer reflection, or even of some less hostile encounters with Jewish inquirers.

The second question had to do with the second coming of Christ. There can be no doubt that when Paul wrote 1 Thessalonians, and indeed 1 Corinthians, he expected this to take place within his own lifetime. Some Christians had already died by the time he wrote; and one of his tasks in writing to the Thessalonians was to reassure them that those who had died would suffer no disadvantage at Christ's coming compared with those who, like himself, would still be alive (4.15). Again, in 1 Corinthians, he describes his own generation as "those on whom the end of the ages has come" (10.11), and clearly distinguishes between those who are already dead and "we" who "shall be changed" (15.52) — that is, those who are still alive. But in later let-ters this expectation seems far less confident; indeed, in Philippians he actu-ally declares himself exercised over the question whether he would do better to resign himself to an imminent death or resolve to save his life if he could (1.21ff.). There is no hint here that he believed the question might in any case be preempted by Christ's return. And in 2 Corinthians, referring to some recent event of a particularly threatening kind (which is most plausi-bly thought to have been a serious illness), he confesses that he "despaired even of remaining alive" (1.8). These were somber and realistic thoughts in the mind of one who had quite recently been confidently assuming he would be one of those who would remain alive to be "caught up in the clouds to meet the Lord in the air" (1 Thess. 4.17).

C. H. Dodd's explanation of this was that, by the time Paul wrote his later letters, the belief among Christians that Christ would return at any moment was already fading, and Paul was merely applying to his own case that more realistic expectation by means of which they were all having to come to terms with the apparent delay of the *parousia*. But this explanation, in its turn, fails to do justice to later texts such as Romans 13.11, "For deliverance is nearer to us now than it was when we first believed," or Philippians 4.5, "The Lord is at hand." The proposition that Paul, or indeed other Christians in his time, ceased to expect an early return of Christ is exceedingly difficult to support from his authentic letters. What changed was his confidence that he would live to see it himself. And this may well have been precipitated by the threatening experience he refers to at the beginning of 2 Corinthians. If he suddenly had to face the possibility of his own death, his confidence that he would be among those who were alive at that crucial moment must have been brutally shaken.

The Charge of Inconsistency

These two instances of an apparent change of mind in Paul's letters have had important consequences for Christian belief and practice. We shall look at one of these in greater detail in a moment. But the important point at this stage is that we are confronted with a body of Scripture which contains statements that are barely compatible with one other and which, taken as the basis for Christian belief and practice, have resulted in widely different attitudes toward, for example, the Jewish people and the meaning and imminence of the second coming of Christ. The presence of these apparent incompatibilities forces us to ask in what sense these writings can be regarded as authoritative. If some Christians can appeal to Paul to justify their belief in, for example, the necessity of converting all Jews to Christ in order to hasten the second coming, or in the absolute immorality of all homosexual acts and orientations, while others are equally confident that Paul would have intended us to show toleration and understanding, both to the Jews and their religion, and (once their true situation is understood) to homosexuals, how can we claim that writings capable of such contrasting interpretations can continue to have authority in the modern world?

In one sense this is not a modern problem at all. It dates, in fact, from the early Christian centuries, when the church undertook the daunting task of expressing Christian doctrine in terms compatible with Greek and Roman logic and philosophy. The problem that the early theologians confronted was that of constructing a logically ordered system of doctrinal propositions out of Scriptures that were not propositional at all. In the case of the gospels, the material was mainly narrative, and offered little foothold for the methods of propositional logic; and in the case of the epistles, it was argumentative, rhetorical, and conditioned by the particular circumstances in which each letter was written. In short, the New Testament, with its pronounced narrative and disputational character, was little adapted to providing the basis of a theological system; and from an early stage philosophy was called in to provide an essential supplement. However, there was a partial exception to this, insofar as Romans, and to a lesser extent Galatians, were recognized as coming nearer to being theological treatises than any other part of the New Testament, and these pages were quarried relentlessly for propositions relating to such concepts as sin, grace, and salvation that could be built into a philosophically respectable system of Christian doctrine. This meant, of course, that the context (and therefore, we might think, important clues to the meaning) of these propositions was disregarded: the fact that Paul had said, for example, that "by Adam came sin," or that "Christ has been sacrificed for us," was sufficient for giving authority to doctrines that had been fashioned as much by philosophical reasoning as by inference from Scripture. By such methods, the basic unsuitability of the Christian Scriptures as the basis for a theological system acceptable to minds trained in Western philosophy and logic seemed to be overcome.

But this, of course, did not come without its price; and the price consisted in fitting everything Paul says elsewhere into this single scheme and ironing out apparent inconsistencies. We must not exaggerate: the task is not necessarily an impossible one, and there are scholars today whose research leads them on critical grounds to present Paul's thought as a seamless whole, just as in earlier centuries theologians found ways to integrate the entire text of his letters into a single theological construction. But to others the enterprise appears forced and artificial. Take two verses of Romans 3. In one, Paul asks, "What advantage has a Jew?" and answers, "Much in many ways." Eight verses later he asks, "Have we, the Jews, any advantage?" and answers, "None whatever." It is true that there are nuances in the text which may be exploited to make the contradiction seem less sharp; and the place of each statement in the argument gives it a somewhat different force. By stressing these factors, interpreters have striven to absolve Paul of inconsistency. Yet it cannot be denied that he has expressed himself in a way that, at the very least, lays him open to the charge of inconsistency and makes it difficult to present a clear statement of his judgment on the status of the Jews in the eyes of God. Attempts to eliminate the apparent contradiction must always arouse the suspicion that the interpreter is anxious at all costs to preserve Paul as an unquestionable authority for Christian truth.

But must his authority depend on the success of this effort? Is it true of any thinker or leader that his or her authority depends on being utterly consistent at all times, never allowing an opinion to develop into something different, and offering a written legacy to subsequent generations of which every word is equally reliable? Certainly this is not how Jesus, Paul, or any of their contemporaries regarded all parts of their Scriptures. Much of the Old Testament could never be regarded as a basis for establishing doctrine or religious truth. True, the Torah (the five books of the Bible) contained a body of legal statutes that were regarded as binding on all Jewish people, and it was axiomatic that every commandment was mandatory. Often, of course, these commandments were found to require interpretation if they were to be carried out in contemporary circumstances, and different schools of thought passed down different legal judgments derived from them. But the Torah's authority as the divine source of the legal code was never in question; every part of it must be observed with equal attention. As regards the prophets and the "writings," on the other hand, these offer a variety of principles and attitudes; indeed, what is stated in one place may well be contradicted in another (the contrast between Qoheleth and Proverbs is a notorious example), and it has been justly observed that the Hebrew Scriptures, taken as a whole, are unique as foundation religious documents in that they contain criticism of themselves. The modern sense of the word "dialectic," meaning a process of reasoning that holds apparently contradictory propositions in tension until they can be brought into a unifying synthesis, is appropriate to much of the Bible; and the same dialectic tradition has continued unabated in Judaism, which in many areas of conduct and belief offers to its observants a record of the debates between learned interpreters which preceded the eventual authoritative judgment. This dialectic character of much of the tradition in no way diminishes the respect in which it is held or the authority it continues to exercise; but it warns us against expecting that the authority and "holiness" of Scripture guarantee that every part of it carries an equally authoritative message.

It follows that, standing within this dialectic tradition, Paul should not be judged as we would judge a Western philosopher, whose surviving work we might expect to be able to condense into a systematic and logically coherent summary. To put it another way: if we accept (as we must) that there were faults and weaknesses in his character, periods of ill health and exasperation in his life, and moments of anger or discouragement in carrying on his mission (one distinguished and learned commentator was prepared to attribute a particularly obscure passage in one of his letters to his "having had a bad night"!), surely we must also accept that he was fallible in intellect as well as body and temperament, and that it would be unrealistic to expect everything he wrote to be uniformly just and true, especially since he wrote within a tradition that was accustomed to the tension between opposing opinions. Christianity is indebted to him (for Jesus said little to this effect) for its generally received doctrine that human beings are, one way or another, all tainted by sin, and that sinlessness is an impossibility for any apart from Jesus himself. This inherent sinfulness has been understood at least since Augustine as radically affecting our power of understanding the things of God and making it forever impossible for us to apprehend the full truth about him. Paul himself acknowledges the strength of his own sinful motivation, and recognizes that he may on occasion have given misplaced emphasis to some statements or provoked misunderstanding by others. This should be a sufficient warning against using any text as "proof" of a doctrine or authorization for a practice; and perhaps we may now ask the question whether his writings, freed from the implication that every word of them must be given equal weight and regarded as an infallible guide to belief and conduct, can be regarded as possessing the authority implied by the designation "Holy Scripture."

But before addressing the question we need to be clear on another: Authority for what? It is obvious enough that we cannot regard him as an authoritative guide to everything he mentions — social conditions in Corinth, for example, or the precise motivations of those adversaries whom he lambasts with such violence. The lesson was learned more than a century ago, in the debate about the Genesis narrative in the light of Darwinian evolution, that the Bible, however authoritative it may be in the sphere of religion, cannot be regarded as a textbook on geology or biology. This lesson surely applies equally to Paul; and we have already seen that in matters of moral conduct he was influenced as much by standards and attitudes prevailing at the time as by distinctively Christian teaching, and that his moral judgments cannot all necessarily be accepted as true for all time. It is important, therefore, to establish where his authority does and does not run. We have already looked at the process by which he came to be regarded as "apostolic" by the early church, and as being therefore authoritative in the Christian community of the time. What we now have to ask is whether, and in what respect, he is still authoritative for us today.

Christians and Jews

A test case is that of the appropriate Christian attitude to the Jewish people. Christians inherit a lamentable history of anti-Semitic polemic, social exclusion, and at times active persecution of the Jews, justified, it was supposed, by certain passages in the gospels such as the crowd's cry of "His blood be on us and on our children" in Matthew's account of the events leading up to the crucifixion (27.25). John's gospel also consistently names the adversaries of Jesus as "the Jews," and though it is possible to read the gospel narrative in a different way so as to exonerate them from the blame for Jesus' innocent death and argue that it was really the Romans who were responsible, it remains true that the great majority of Jews at the time who came into any contact with Jesus rejected his claim to be messiah, and their leaders' opposition to him cannot but have been a major factor in his condemnation. Nevertheless, at this early stage, all his followers were, like him, Jews themselves, and their immediate impulse was not so much to cry out for the punishment of their fellow Jews as to invite them to penitence and conversion. Indeed, it seemed to many Christians that due punishment was soon inflicted on them by God through the catastrophe of 70 C.E., when the temple in Jerusalem was destroyed and Jews were expelled from the holy city. But a new factor came into play very soon after the crucifixion. Though in its first years the church evidently felt at home in the temple precincts and (apart from certain episodes judged to be subversive) was tolerated by the Jewish authorities, attitudes very soon hardened on both sides and the Christians found themselves the objects of active persecution — not least by Paul himself before his conversion. Then, when the adherence of Gentiles to the new churches aroused further Jewish animosity, persecution sharpened and seemed to justify the strong language we have already commented on in 1 Thessalonians. Taking its cue from this prominent strand in the New Testament record, the church for many centuries seldom felt compunction in authorizing its members to share in public manifestations of anti-Semitism.

But the Nazi policy toward Jews in Germany in the years leading up to the Second World War, and the horrors of the Holocaust in which it resulted, profoundly influenced Christian attitudes. Not merely was there a massive wave of sympathy and compassion for the victims, and a determination that such a crime against humanity should never be committed again (resulting, for instance, in the Universal Declaration of Human Rights in 1948), but Christians had the uncomfortable feeling that their traditional sense of justified animosity toward the Jews, along with the perverse influence of another text taken out of context in Romans (13.1, "Every person must submit to the authorities in power") which had for centuries been the basis of the traditional Lutheran reluctance to interfere in public life, had in some degree contributed to German acquiescence in a ruthless policy of extermination. This feeling was particularly acute in Germany itself, where it made scholars focus their attention on those passages in the New Testament which evinced a more positive attitude toward the Jewish people. The prime text for consideration in this light was Paul's discussion of the place of the Jewish people in the purposes of God, worked out at length in three chapters of Romans (9–11) — the longest consecutive treatment of a single topic in any of Paul's letters. Indeed, the ability to interpret this passage along lines favorable to contemporary Jewry became almost a touchstone of orthodoxy in Protestant scholarly circles.

In this passage Paul tackled a question which, as he confessed himself, had caused him great anguish: Gentiles, along with Jews, had been admitted into the Christian church, the "New Israel." What then was the destiny in the purposes of God of those who, until his conversion to Christianity, had been his colleagues, neighbors, and friends? He was now forced to believe that, by their rejection of Jesus Christ, they had forfeited their claim to salvation. Did this mean that what had seemed their eternal destiny of being God's chosen people had now been rescinded? Had the immense promises made again and again in their scriptures now been cancelled? Had the magnificent Jewish inheritance of inspired writings, sanctified law, and exalted moral aspirations now come to nothing? Paul could not accept such a conclusion, however much it seemed logically entailed by his own argument. His solution was to look at the question in the long term. It must indeed be true that the present rejection of Christ by the Jews excluded them from enjoying the favor of God; but the very progress of the gospel, with its welcome to Gentiles as well as Jews, would ultimately result in a responsiveness on the part of the Jewish people that would bring them to make up the "full complement" (Paul's metaphor in 11.12, suggesting the crew of a ship) of those who were assured of salvation.

The Jewish people, then, were not, as Paul had previously maintained, eternally condemned to retribution for the death of Christ; their destiny as a chosen people would be fulfilled, but in a different fashion from that which had been accepted before: they would form a new, integrated entity with the Christian community of believers, accepted and sanctified together by the impartial gift of God's saving grace. Read in this light, Romans 9–11 became a charter for a new Christian attitude toward the Jews, one of respect and even affection as ultimate partners in a divinely favored destiny. The necessary penitence felt by Christians for previous judgments that may have contributed to the horror of the Holocaust could now be followed by a new openness to the prospect of an eventual reconciliation; and the authority for this change in perception was none other than that of Paul himself.

But even this advance in moral sensitivity did not come without a price. The assumption behind Paul's tortuous argument was that, since the resistance shown by the Jews in the face of the gospel would not persist forever, it was essential that this gospel should continue to be preached to them unremittingly. They must never be in the position of asking how they could have heard of it. "How could they hear without someone to spread the news? And how could anyone spread the news without being sent?" (Rom. 10.14-15). This seems to imply that a "mission to the Jews," seeking to persuade and convert them to Christianity, remains an absolute imperative for Christians to this day. But we are now in an era when interfaith relations are based on a quite different premise. Respect for other religions is seen to imply an abandonment of deliberate proselytism from members of other faiths. Mutual understanding and cooperation are jeopardized when there is an explicit intention to convert. These chapters of Romans may be of immense value in encouraging a new understanding of the ultimate destiny of the Jewish people from a Christian perspective; but they have to be set aside when it comes to the question of whether it is appropriate to evangelize them. The authority of Paul is gratefully acknowledged in the one case; in the other it has to be uneasily set aside.

Is this necessarily selective appeal to Paul's authority fatal to the claim that the Scriptures which contain his writings are holy, authoritative, and true? As we have seen, this was certainly not the view of those who first began to retrieve and make a collection of his correspondence with his churches and to place it alongside both the gospels and the Old Testament as "Scripture." Indeed, the fact that they did so is itself of considerable significance. Paul's letters, after all, were just that: the response of an individual pastor and evangelist to particular issues that had arisen in early Christian congregations, formulated according to the epistolary conventions of the time, occasionally tinged with personal anger, anxiety, or impatience, and bearing the imprint of an often pugnacious personality. We are a world away from the sentences of serene wisdom which fill the pages of the holy books of most world religions. At times, too, their meaning was far from clear and their ambiguities were liable to be exploited by heretics, as is noted in the one subsequent reference to them which we find in the New Testament (2 Pet. 3.16). Yet in that same reference, within half a century of their being written, they are already referred to as "Scripture." It is unlikely that, when he wrote them, Paul had any inkling that they would come to be regarded in this way, or indeed that he had any intention of their being preserved indefinitely for general use in the churches. That they so rapidly achieved this status may have been partly due to his insistent claim — vigorously contested at the time, but subsequently universally accepted in the church — that he was an "apostle" on an equal footing with the other apostles; hence it could be said that his writings deserved the prestigious label "apostolic." It may be partly due also to the crucial role he played in spreading the gospel in Gentile regions and founding churches in Asia Minor, Greece, and beyond — though the most important of these, the church in Rome, had already been founded by the time he reached it. But these factors, though they certainly enhanced Paul's significance in the history of the church, could not in themselves have promoted him to the rank of author of Holy Scripture. It was evidently the quality of what he wrote, his pioneering application of the gospel he had received to new circumstances, and the testimony his letters gave to the experience of a man seized with the enthusiasm and inspiration of the very first generation of Christians which left early readers in no doubt that in them they possessed writings that, despite all their obscurity, their references to particular circumstances that had now passed, and their occasionally intemperate language, could nevertheless be revered as authoritative guides to belief and conduct in the foreseeable future: they were "Scripture."

What Kind of Authority?

This early acceptance of Paul's letters into the canon of Scripture gives us a clue to the nature of the authority which they possessed and indeed may still possess for Christians. They offer an intensely personal record of a crucial phase in the evolution of faith in Jesus Christ from its origins in a small group of followers in Jerusalem to a network of believers spreading as far as the center of the Roman empire. A man of brilliant intellect, sophisticated education, and immense determination and stamina, Paul labored over a period of nearly thirty years to bring his intense personal experience of Jesus Christ into close interaction, both with the memories and traditions preserved by the Jerusalem apostles and with the entirely new problems posed by the attempts at a life of discipleship being made by newly converted Christians in the very different culture of the wider Greco-Roman world. As such, he offered a template against which subsequent generations of evangelists, pastors, and church administrators could measure their efforts and monitor their methods. There was no other model of comparable authority by which they could be guided. It was therefore understandable that, along with somewhat similar, though less powerful and extensive, alleged relics of the correspondence of other apostles (James, Peter, Judas, and John), these writings, which had begun life as occasional pieces written for particular purposes, were found to be irreplaceable sources of reference and inspiration for church congregations and their ministers, and became, along with the gospels, one of the principal components of the collection which the church was to recognize by the end of the second century as its "Holy Scripture": the New Testament.

CHAPTER 7

Supplying "as if"

—❦—

"**A** re you the one who is to come, or are we to wait for another?"
(Matt. 11.3). This question, asked of Jesus by John the Baptist's disciples, tells us something very significant about the culture in which Jesus lived and about its understanding of time and history. When they read their Scriptures, Jesus' fellow Jews took it for granted that they could find precursors and pointers in the past relating to significant events and persons that would be encountered in the present or the near future. The phrase, "one who is to come," implied a view of history, of providence, and of a divine purpose in events as they unfolded; and this was in stark contrast to the assumptions of their pagan neighbors. It was a contrast of which the author of Acts was fully aware, and, as we shall see, his account of Paul's speech to the Athenians on the Areopagus is an instructive example of a clash of cultures with which Christians needed to come to terms if they were to persuade pagans of the truth of the gospel.

This contrast did not consist in the fact that the Bible contained "prophecies" which its readers believed would certainly be "fulfilled"; for this was a belief also held by pagans. Throughout the ancient world respect was paid to "prophets" of the past: prophetic figures, and indeed prophetic books, allegedly from the remote past, were regularly consulted for enlightenment about the probable outcome of contemporary events and policies. And not only prophecies: an ancient tradition of "wisdom," which implied an understanding of the probable future consequences of present conduct and policies, was a common possession of the civilized world, and was drawn on by pagan philosophers and moralists, just as it underlay the maxims ascribed to Solomon. The difference came in the view of history implied by phrases such as "the one who is to come."

Paul in Athens

For the Greeks and Romans, history was a succession of chance events, even if molded, certainly, by great leaders with the aid, or at least the compliance, of the gods. If duly chronicled, this history might be of value for contemporary generals and statesmen, in that lessons could be learned from the failures and successes of the past. Such instruction was the explicit aim of Thucydides, even if most of his successors wrote mainly to glorify certain individuals or nations, or to offer interest and entertainment to their readers. If history had any shape or purpose, this was sometimes seen as a continual decline from an original golden age. Such an age might conceivably be restored by the propitious advent of a gifted ruler (an expectation voiced in Virgil's 4th Eclogue); and some philosophers (but probably not many other people) also believed that the physical world was of limited duration and would be brought to an end — though not necessarily in the near future — by a cosmic cataclysm. Moreover, that the world had been created by God, and was divinely adapted to the needs of human beings, was a widely shared belief, and in addressing the people of Athens, Paul (at least in Luke's presentation of his approach in Acts 17) was able to enlist his hearers' interest by affirming this belief as the common possession of Jews and pagans. But it is significant that Paul did not go on to argue that God played any part in the progress of his creation other than by remaining "close" to the human beings he had created (17.27). Certainly, that human beings will have to give an account of themselves to their creator after death was widely believed, and if taken seriously this belief implied a challenge to repent of evil deeds. That such judgment was an imminent possibility for every individual (one's death might come at any time) was also a frequent theme of moralists. But when Paul went on to speak of a particular "day" which God had determined for the (presumably simultaneous) judgment of "the whole world," he was introducing an idea that was entirely foreign to his hearers, and it is significant that then, for the first time in the speech, he relapsed into biblical language drawn from the Psalms. It is no surprise that when he went on to connect this judgment with a certain individual's "resurrection from the dead," they became incredulous — though a few were intrigued.

Strikingly absent from this speech is any suggestion that a key to understanding the present might be found in events or persons of the past or that this person who had been "raised from the dead" was one who "was to come"; he was simply "a man whom God appointed" as a herald, or possibly an initiator, of imminent judgment — just as it might be said that the gods had indicated the future achievements of Alexander the Great by certain supernatural phenomena at his birth. Luke carefully represents Paul as speaking to a pagan audience whose conception of history was quite different from his own and as adapting his message so far as possible to their culture, saying nothing about significant past events or divinely ordained outcomes: such ideas which would have been foreign to them. By contrast, when addressing Jewish people, or Gentiles familiar with the Jewish culture (which is what we must assume his "God-fearer" converts to have been), Paul is reported to have adopted a quite different strategy, seeking to persuade them that the pattern of Israel's history as recorded in their Scriptures pointed to the providential nature of recent events: the crucifixion and resurrection of Jesus had been foretold and had happened according to the preordained purposes of God. For them, that is to say, it was natural to think that history was moving toward a divinely intended culmination, and that events in the past could be studied as precursors of what was soon to take place. "Searching the scriptures" was a necessary activity for understanding the present and the near future, complemented by "reading the signs of the times" to determine how far the divinely ordained scenario had progressed. Paul himself (or whoever wrote Rom. 16.25 and Ephesians, where the phrase occurs several times) was to call this process "the revealing of the mystery" of God's purposes, dimly apprehended before but now fully intelligible in the light of the Christian experience.

But there was also a radically new feature in this understanding of history. It was not just that the state of creation was self-evidently imperfect and failed to reflect the just purposes of the Creator, who surely intended a more glorious destiny for it sometime in the future. This moment of restoration and renewal was now imminent; indeed, there were already signs of its actualization. From the very first recorded preaching of Jesus — "the Kingdom of heaven is at hand" — and right through the New Testament period, there is the same note of urgency. History had reached a critical phase in the great design of God. A change was imminent that would affect all human beings, and deliverance was available for all who would accept it. Among Jesus' own people the idea was not strange: messianic expectation was a feature of the culture. But this was a significant variant: the agent of the expected restoration would be of a nature — nonviolent, poor, persecuted, and ultimately executed — that no one could have envisaged, even if there had been hints of it, seldom appreciated, in the prophetic writings. That this variant was indeed within God's saving purposes had now been decisively validated by a single event, the mention of which was too much for Paul's audience in Athens: the resurrection of Jesus from the dead.

What we have in the Areopagus speech, therefore, is not just the shocking intrusion of a singular individual and a singular event into a discourse which Paul's hearers expected to consist of generalized concepts of philosophy and religion; it is the confrontation of two very different ways of looking at history. Pagan historians, though they professed to regard reporting the truth about events of the past as their first priority, nevertheless recognized the necessity of offering some interpretation of those events and drawing from them lessons which would benefit those with responsibility for the present. Some, indeed, went further than this and detected some underlying pattern in the succession of historical epochs, the rise and fall of empires, and the successes and failures of political and military leaders. The mythology of an original golden age which might one day return, the philosophical notion of a cyclical sequence of creation, decay, and re-creation spread over many centuries, the likelihood of acts of hubris leading inevitably to some form of nemesis — all these were invoked to give some sense and order to the mass of disparate facts from the past with which the historian had to deal. But the historiography of the Hebrew Scriptures (challenged only in one instance by Qoheleth's insistence that "there is nothing new under the sun"), and the characteristic Jewish understanding of their own past, was quite different.

For the Jew, it was taken for granted that lessons were to be learned, not by discerning the causes of historical events and sequences, but by recognizing their place in the divinely ordained purposes of God. True, the Deuteronomists' explanation of catastrophes in the history of Jerusalem — that they were the consequence of gross impiety and idolatry on the part of the kings — was not unlike the pattern of hubris and nemesis detected by pagan historians; but it also differed fundamentally, in that every reverse in the fortunes of the people of Israel was set in the context of a relationship with God which was believed to be ultimately unbreakable and must result in a glorious destiny sometime in the future. To put it in another way: the Greek and Roman study of history was an expression of their intellectual culture. The task was to interpret individual events as illustrating general principles, to draw from particulars lessons that could be applied universally. By contrast, the entire Jewish culture was focused on one particular nation in one particular place, within which a small number of individuals had a unique significance. In the Old Testament it is very rare indeed for there to be any sense of a need to understand history outside national boundaries (the appearance of what looks like a "natural law" shared with other nations in Amos 1–2 is a rare example). When the destiny of other nations is mentioned, it is simply to illustrate the inevitable retribution which must fall upon the idolatrous enemies and oppressors of Israel and the example it may one day set to them of the true worship and service of the one God. Far from exemplifying general truths, the events of the past were seen as stages in the divinely ordained progress of a particular people toward a promised destiny. The kingdoms of this world, in Daniel's vision, would all necessarily be short-lived and give way to the eternal Kingdom of God, in which the righteous people of Israel would inherit their honored place.

Biblical Expectancy

Integral to this understanding of the past was therefore a constant expectation regarding the future. God holds firm to a purpose and a destiny for his chosen people, which may be delayed because of their inevitable failure to match their conduct to his moral and religious requirements but which will assuredly come to pass within the time span allotted to world history. Past events and the vagaries of human character and policy may be understood as impeding or promoting the divine purposes. More than this, the Bible contains hints, particularly in the prophetic writings, of a pattern of development which may be expected to recur and which should therefore be watched for as a sign that the present stage of history presages an acceleration toward the ultimate dénouement. As we have seen, some believed that the crucial stage would be initiated and facilitated by an individual — a messiah — such as was dimly prefigured in certain scriptural texts and came to be given a more definite profile in popular belief; others placed more confidence in the prospect of a general change of heart such as was prophesied by Jeremiah. But it was taken for granted by all that one could legitimately "search the scriptures" for precursors of significant developments in the present, and even expect that some outstanding individual from the past — such as one who might be called "son of" (i.e., with all the good and exceptional qualities of) David — would return to initiate the new era: he would be "the one who was to come."

But far more was at stake here than an academic attitude to history. It is not sufficiently often noticed that one of the most frequent characterizations of Christians in the New Testament is that they are "waiting." What precisely they are "waiting" for — whether the return of Christ, the coming of the Kingdom, or the announcement of the day of final reckoning — may be left on one side for the moment. The important point is that they are living *in expectation.* It is not the case, for them, that every day can be assumed to be much the same as the one before, that their life will inevitably consist of the same struggles against disease and misfortune, the same satisfactions from home, family, and material well-being, the same falling into sin, the same striving after righteousness, as it always has done. On the contrary, their entire strategy for life, nourished by the promises of their new religion, is based on the expectation of something different in the near or not-too-distant future. We have already seen how this note of urgent expectancy gave impetus and relevance to the moral teaching of Jesus. But this sense of living on the threshold of a new age reached into every aspect of personal existence: it fundamentally relativized the present age. If one accepted that "the time we live in will not last long. . . . [T]he world as we know it is passing away" (1 Cor. 7.29-31), then material possessions, social ties, ethnic and national identity, and all worldly concerns became of lesser importance. It is no exaggeration to say that this quality of "waiting" was a keynote of the Christian life. There were some (we learn from 2 Thess. 2.2) who believed that the "Day of the Lord" had arrived, that the Christian experience was already complete. They had a new philosophy of life, a new experience of the Spirit, and there was nothing further to wait for. These people had to be sternly corrected. True, they had come into possession of new spiritual depths and experiences, but this did not mean that they should give up the vital expectation of a future divine "Kingdom" existentially different from the present. Equally, those who began to doubt any significant change in the future, even to the point of denying any "resurrection from the dead," were left with little value to set on life other than "to eat and drink, for tomorrow we die" (1 Cor. 15.32).

Thus, "waiting for the revelation of the Lord Jesus Christ" (1 Cor. 1.7) is a phrase which succinctly describes the worldview and recommended lifestyle of the first generations of Christians. Indeed, one New Testament author, writing probably late in the first century, roundly attacked those who appeared to be questioning the reality of this expectation (2 Pet. 3.4ff.). What this "coming" meant, and how they would describe this expectation, inevitably varied a good deal. What lay in the future, according to Paul, was the "revelation" of the Lord, or of Christians' sonship, or of ultimate "justification" — a type of expectation that seems to be validated by reports in the gospels of Jesus prophesying the "coming" of the Son of man in glory. For the most part, Jesus himself was less explicit about the shape of what was to come, preferring to speak in allusive terms or in parables about the "Kingdom"; but he did so with consistent urgency, and this urgency was faithfully reflected in the exhortations and missionary activity of his followers. To be vigilant, sober, prepared, and equipped for the promised future, whatever precisely that might be, was inherent in the calling to be a Christian.

As the years passed, was this expectation disappointed? Did the Christian hope fade? Did the reality of history that was evidently continuing on its accustomed course displace the early enthusiasm for expected change? New Testament scholars have persistently searched for signs of a slackening of the intensity of hopes for the future. Paul, as we have seen, is sometimes suspected of having given up expecting an early *parousia;* Acts is thought to betray a deliberate attempt by its author to emphasize the degree to which promises of a new, Spirit-filled age were already being fulfilled in the early church, allowing him to relegate expectations of an actual return of Christ to a distant and unpredictable future. But it has to be said that signs of any such reinterpretation in the early period are exceedingly faint. What is more striking is the extent to which the church appears to have adjusted to the prospect of a longer time-scale of history without in any way losing its fervor or its confidence. As the first generation of Christians died out and their successors too began to face the likelihood of dying before any radical change took place, it might have been expected that strains would have begun to show in the whole fabric of their belief. But in fact it appears that so vivid was their consciousness of new possibilities in life, of a new, Spirit-inspired energy and capacity to transform individual lives, and of unprecedented resources for patience and endurance even under persecution, that the necessary lengthening of historical perspective seems to have caused little in the way of upset to the firm conviction that the future was in God's hands and that the church had been given a crucial role in the evolution of the present toward its ordained destiny. Even the passage already referred to from 2 Peter, which has often been appealed to as evidence of a slackening of expectation, does not necessarily bear this interpretation.

2 Peter

It is worth giving this passage some attention, for it well illustrates the tension we have been discerning between two very different views of history and the expected future. The author (who is usually presumed to be writing late in the first century) is answering the "scoffers" who are casting doubt on "the promise of his *parousia.*" "Still everything goes on exactly as it always has done since the world began" (3.4) — this was the normal way of looking at things for any philosophically inclined pagan: history may tend to repeat itself, but it has no radical surprises in store. The Christians are surely deluding themselves if they seriously expect an altogether new state of affairs to come about in the near future. That the author has to address this question for his Christian readers is usually taken as an indication that Christianity was having to adjust itself to a new phase: the first generation of Christians was passing away, but still the promised *parousia* of Christ had shown no signs of appearing. Believers were therefore vulnerable to "scoffers" who mocked them for a faith that was being shown to rest on a false promise; and once the sense of urgency had gone out of the religion, there might well follow a decline in moral alertness and sobriety — these scoffers could be accused of living "self-indulgent lives" (3.3).

But if this was the question at issue, the author's reply seems somewhat beside the point. He reminds his readers that heaven and earth, having been originally constituted out of water, were destined to perish by the element of fire at the moment of final judgment and sentencing of the impious. This is hardly an answer to the question of the delay of Christ's return. But what exactly was this *parousia* that they denied? They could perfectly well have meant by the word *parousia* — or at least this author could have taken them to mean — the coming of the ultimate "Day of God"; and this was generally expected to involve the final judgment of all human beings and the dissolution of the physical universe. This expectation of the future was of course vulnerable to philosophical skepticism; but there was a significant hint of it in the Old Testament. It was very widely believed, in the east as well as the west, that the end of the present world order, when it came, would take place through a cataclysm of water and fire. Read the book of Genesis, and you could see that part of this had already taken place — or very nearly taken place — in the time of Noah: it was only through God's forbearance and favor toward a single just man that total destruction through water had been averted. Nevertheless, this was the first phase of the final cataclysm. What remained was the fire, and this could now come at any time. Unlike the philosophers, Jewish and Christian people had reason to think that the dénouement might be quite imminent. On this basis there were no grounds for scoffing.

The author then goes on to a second argument. "With the Lord one day is like a thousand years, and a thousand years are like one day" (3.8). In modern religious thought this is almost a truism. Of course, we say, God's time-scale is totally different from ours: what seems to us like a delay of many years is to God the mere blink of an eye. But this again ignores the presuppositions that the author's readers would have held. Few people in antiquity expected world history to continue indefinitely. So far it had lasted (most people believed) some three or four thousand years. How much longer would it continue? An answer commonly given supposed a total duration of history (or at least of this phase of it: some believed it went in recurring cycles) of seven thousand years. But Jewish people had a special reason for refining this estimate. According to Genesis, God created the world in six days, and this could be read as symbolic of the divine arithmetic: "one day is like a thousand years," an interpretation apparently confirmed by the words which the author quotes from Psalm 90, "a thousand years are like one day." Thus Scripture revealed that creation was based on a seven-day "week": six thousand years was the maximum for world history; the seventh thousand — the "sabbath rest" — would be an altogether new epoch, preceded by the general judgment of humankind. Given this timescale, history still had at least some hundreds of years to run: there was no room for scoffing that the end had not yet come. But at the same time one could not be sure. The promised *parousia* of Christ might accelerate the program, and God might shorten the days for the sake of his elect. Be vigilant, therefore, for it might come "like a thief" (3.10).

Is History Going Anywhere?

If this is the correct interpretation, it reveals very clearly a profound difference of perception between Jews and Christians on the one hand and those influenced, even remotely, by Greco-Roman philosophy on the other. For the latter, it made little sense to talk of any kind of *parousia*, if by this was meant some form of divine intervention or revelation expected to occur as the destined culmination of world history. Events, for them, succeeded one another without any clear purpose or direction; at most one could discern factors in human affairs which, each time they appeared, were liable to make for failure or success, wealth or poverty, opportunity or oppression. Amid the succession of apparently random and barely predictable historical outcomes the best recipe for happiness, according to the reigning philosophy, was to cultivate detachment from all emotions that such vicissitudes arouse and bring the rational part of one's personality into harmony with a universe itself perceived to be founded and governed on rational principles. Hence the "scoffers"; hence the contempt felt by a pagan such as Celsus in the third century for what he saw as the pretentious probing of the past and the delusive expectations of the future indulged in by Christians and Jews in the interests of enhancing their own significance on the wide canvas of world history (Origen, *Contra Celsum* 4.23). Those, by contrast, whose attitude to these things was formed by the Bible felt themselves to be in a totally different relationship with both the past and the future. In the past they could find evidence of the working out of God's purposes for the world, focused as these purposes were on the destiny of God's own peculiar people, as well as reliable clues to the shape of things to come; in the future they could look forward with confidence to "new heavens and a new earth, in which justice will be established" (2 Pet. 3.13). Indeed, it was impossible to understand the Bible at all without acquiescing in this purposive view of history, a view that would inevitably invite the "scoffing" of a reflective pagan.

This profound cultural difference was undoubtedly an obstacle which had to be overcome when the first Christian missionaries sought to persuade pagans of the truth of their message. In the centuries that followed, Christian thinkers adopted a number of strategies for making their view of history credible to those who saw it in terms which today we would call "secular." In the fourth century, after the conversion of Constantine and the christianization of the Roman empire, the church's first systematic historian, Eusebius of Caesarea, interpreted the future hope of God's Kingdom as already realized when Christianity became the religion of the world's greatest empire, an interpretation which remained dominant in the east throughout the Byzantine period. In the fifth century, after the sack of Rome by the Goths, which was blamed by many of its citizens on its abandonment of its traditional religion in favor of Christianity, Augustine propounded a quite different reading of world history according to which the Roman empire receded in significance, being subject to the inevitable vicissitudes of all human political structures. The only lasting reality — the City of God — existed outside history, impacting upon it in mysterious ways but fully to be realized only in God's own time in the future. Down the centuries these two views of history remained in tension with each other. At certain times the Eusebian view seemed to be validated by the emergence of great "Christian" empires: the Spanish discoveries and missionary enterprise in South America made sixteenth-century Spain seem for a while like the agent of the destined culmination of history. Bossuet argued in the same terms for the reign of Louis XIV of France. Victorian Britain, with its expanding empire that seemed to be bringing Christianity, along with civilization, to primitive peoples in distant continents, encouraged a similar sense of historical fulfillment; while the advance of science and the immense improvements in physical welfare which followed it made it seem irrational to think that the world had any greater destiny to look forward to. Such confidence was of course finally shattered in the twentieth century by two world wars and the atrocities that attended them, leaving only the choice, it seemed, between an otherworldly millenarianism such as is promoted by certain religious sects and the negatively pragmatic view of historical events characteristic of postmodernism.

Is this our choice today? Must we either take the Bible seriously, and therefore commit ourselves to what (after two thousand years) cannot but seem to be a hopelessly naive expectation of world history being suddenly brought to an end, or at least transformed, by a decisive act of God; or else must we be prepared to declare that, in this respect at least, we can no longer regard the Jewish and Christian Scriptures as either authoritative or relevant for our time? And since the biblical authors' view of time and history was so integral to their message, would not this second alternative be tantamount to confessing that we can no longer regard them as privileged communicators of a transcendent message? Would it not forever disqualify the Bible from being called "Holy"?

Registers of Language

I believe there are two reasons why we should not think we are now shut up to these bleak alternatives. It is true that those who still adhere most faithfully to the prospect of some imminent *parousia* are mainly members of fundamentalist sects whose conclusions — Armageddon within this generation, a new era for the elect, possibly focused on a restored State of Israel — would be repudiated by the great majority of Christians in the world. But this is surely not the only way of taking the biblical view of history seriously. European culture and European languages have tended to make a clear distinction between what is actually the case and what it may be compared with. We like to make it entirely clear whether we mean that such and such a thing actually happened or that it was "as if" such and such a thing had happened. We have a variety of figures of speech — metaphors, similes, analogies, and so forth — which enable us to describe things in the real world in terms of other things; but when we do so, there is seldom any doubt about what we are doing. If we say that "the sun set on our hopes," we do not imagine for a moment that this experience had anything to do with the time of day when we abandoned hope. But the Hebrew tradition, reflected again and again in the New Testament writings, used metaphor and comparison with far greater freedom. "My mouth is dry as a potsherd, and my tongue sticks to my gums" (Ps. 22.15) is easily recognizable as a precise, almost clinical, description of a physical condition. But a few verses earlier we read, "A herd of bulls surrounds me, great bulls of Bashan beset me." We might well imagine, when we first read this verse, that the psalmist has found himself in a stretch of unguarded pastureland and is faced with the acute danger of attack by a herd of bulls. It is only when we read on that we realize that this is metaphor. The psalmist's actual trouble is acute illness. Similarly, when the gospels report that at the moment of Jesus' death on the cross "the curtain of the temple was torn in two from top to bottom," the sentence is written in exactly the same form as the preceding one, which is a clear statement of fact: "Then Jesus gave a loud cry and died" (Mark 15.37). Accordingly, the modern reader is tempted to assume that the two sentences belong to the same linguistic register. Both record facts; therefore, the curtain was literally torn in two. But there seems little doubt that this is a misreading. An actual rending of the massive curtain which hung over the temple door would have been a freakish and extraordinary occurrence that would surely have been commented on elsewhere, and even if it did take place there would have been no way of establishing that it had happened simultaneously with the moment of Jesus' death outside the city. There can be little doubt, therefore, that the report is metaphorical — it was *as if* the curtain had been torn, meaning that by the death of Jesus the separation between God and human beings, symbolized by the curtain concealing the sacred part of the temple, had been decisively overcome; and this interpretation is confirmed by the use of the same metaphor by the author of the Letter to Hebrews — "the new and living way which he has opened for us through the curtain, the way of his flesh" (10.20). The modern reader is misled by the two sentences having exactly the same grammatical form, being in the same linguistic register. In both cases we would now say, "It was *as if* a herd of bulls . . . ," "It was *as if* the curtain. . . ." But biblical writers saw less need of helping the reader in this way. They assumed that the *as if* would be supplied in the reader's mind.

But they could also assume that the reader (or the hearer) would know when *not* to supply "as if." That is to say, the prime function of language is to convey information, and it can do so effectively only if it is clearly understood when words are being used in their literal sense to state what is or was the case. The speaker with an immediate practical message cannot leave it to chance whether the hearer takes the words literally or metaphorically: the response being called for by this act of speech is to recognize the true state of affairs and act accordingly. But language also has many other functions, one of which is to alert the hearer's or reader's imagination to possibilities and similarities that might not be immediately apparent. For this, it has a number of resources. There are similes, which make the comparison explicit: "My love is like a red, red rose"; but there are also metaphors, and these require the hearer to make a new connection. "All the world's a stage" — we see at once that this is not a literal description of the terrestrial structure, and are forced to look for another meaning, assisted in this case by the fact that the theater offers itself as an obvious replica of real life. Yes, of course, we say, that is just what the world (in some respects) is like; and we follow the poet's elaboration of the theme without any doubt as to his meaning. On the other hand, if we hear that "all the world is subject to climate change," we shall not think for a moment that this is merely metaphorical: it is becoming a matter of established fact.

In other words, the indications that language is being used metaphorically and not literally may be many and subtle. When a story is being told to us, we shall want to make up our minds whether it is true or fictional. But we shall also need to make other judgments — not only *did* it happen, but *could* it have happened? Is the story so improbable as to be deliberately grotesque or comic? Is it a fairy story or an allegory? Are the events symbolic or mythical, leading the mind to grasp more general realities? And to make these judgments we need the assistance of the cultural tradition within which the story is told. We need to be able to follow the clues — which are often quite subtle — provided by literary genre, verbal allusion, linguistic style, and intended audience. If a paragraph begins with the words, "It is reliably reported that . . . ," we know we have to take seriously the facts it contains. But if it begins, "Once upon a time . . . ," we shall assume that it is a fairy story and be ready to withhold belief. And part of the artifice of sophisticated writers and playwrights may be to keep us in suspense over the idiom they are using. Is Ionesco's "rhinoceros" really in the next room or only in the imagination of the characters? Is the occasional fantasy of Charles Williams's or Algernon Blackwood's stories, or the *realismo magico* of some recent Latin American novelists, a mere flight of fancy, or is it meant to make us think that such things could actually happen and reflect on the consequences of their possible happening? As William Blake wrote, "Everything possible to be believed is an image of truth." A certain ambiguity may be part of a literary repertoire; to appreciate it we need to be familiar with the idiom and the culture. And this is precisely our difficulty when we come to the Bible. Much of the time there is little doubt about the linguistic register being used. "It came to pass in the days of . . ." clearly introduces what purports to be a factual report. "The Kingdom of heaven is like . . ." clearly introduces a comparison. But there are borderline cases. What sort of stories were Jesus' parables? On one occasion his hearers saw a particular purpose: when Jesus told the parable of the wicked laborers in the vineyard, the authorities "saw that the parable was aimed at them" (Mark 12.12). Is this true of other parables, or of all of them? Did they generally have a target, a particular intention? Were they allegories, in which each character stood for someone or something else? Were they sharp anecdotes with just one point of reference? These questions have been debated for many years and are still not fully resolved. And the reason is simply that we do not have all the clues which would have been available to the original hearers and would have enabled them to seize Jesus' intentions more easily.

If this is true with relatively familiar genres of speaking and writing such as stories that are told to illustrate a principle or press home a point — like

Jesus' parables — how much more must it be true when the discourse adopts a form that is far less at home in our culture. Today, when we speak about the future, our language and imagery are normally a projection of past or present experience. If we are optimistic, we imagine a scenario in which all that is good in our history becomes the resource for a new era of peace, justice, and prosperity; if we are pessimists, we imagine past ills being intensified in the future. But we seldom relate our thinking, as the biblical writers were bound to do, to the postulates of a profound conviction that the universe was created by God, that it is not yet, in its present state, as he intended it to be, and that he will infallibly bring into being a new era of righteousness and rightful reward. How was this confidently expected future to be put into words? It was certainly not a case for factual description and precise coordinates of time and place. The promised reality would not be a replica of what had already been experienced. History provided neither the materials for constructing a template of the future nor a calendar for its accomplishment. To present it to the imagination of hearers and readers, ordinary language needed to be stretched to its limits. Simile and metaphor, paradox and even apparent contradiction, must be brought into play. And this the audience would be well aware of. If the discourse was directed to these future realities, they would not expect factual reporting. They would be prepared for analogies and comparisons, for an appeal to imagination, not an exercise in prediction. In short, when offered a scenario of the divinely purposed future, they would instinctively supply the qualification *as if*.

It follows that when we are confronted in the Bible with what appear to be dramatic scenarios of an imminently unfolding future, we need to make a similar adjustment. Rather than asking why these forecasts have not been literally fulfilled, or whether, in view of their nonfulfillment, we must question the credibility and authority of the biblical writers, we must ask whether we have correctly understood the idiom they are using. Are they saying that a certain dénouement *will* take place within just a few years, or are they saying that the reality is not such as can be pinned down in any precise forecasting: the nearest we can get to it is to say it will be *as if* it were imminent? For this, in the Hebrew culture, was never an academic question, as it was, say, for Stoic philosophers. For practical purposes Marcus Aurelius's view of the future was typical: "It is impossible for it to escape the pattern of the present" (7.49). If, as some believed, there was to be a cyclical dissolution of the existing world order, the only question was whether this was more likely to occur within a thousand or two thousand years. But in the Bible the future scenario was a matter of critical importance. It impinged upon the present. It involved judgment, the apportionment of just reward and condign punishment and the fulfillment of promises of national regeneration that each generation had some responsibility for setting forward. Only if these expectations were kept alive could human conduct be fully motivated toward the good. It was the promised future which must orient earnest living in the present. And this affected the language in which this future must be described. Of course, no one could say precisely when it would come to pass — though the "signs of the times" might seem to justify a high level of alert. But it would rob the message of its relevance if the time-scale were left entirely vague. It would not do to allow it to recede into an indefinite future. Equally, present activity should not be paralyzed by dire warnings of apocalypse tomorrow. To have the necessary impact on the present, the scenario must always be presented *as if* within the lifetime of its hearers, or at least their children — that is, *soon!*

Receiving the Message

This sense of urgent expectation was in stark contrast to the normal assumptions of pagan culture. The Roman historian Polybius was typical of his time when he wrote,

> A regular course is appointed by nature in which constitutions change, are transformed, and finally return to their original state. Anyone who clearly perceives this may perhaps be wrong in his estimate of the time the process will take, but . . . he will seldom be mistaken as regards the stage of growth or decline at which a past constitution has arrived or the point at which it will undergo some change. (6.9.10)

For their part, the biblical writers saw history from a quite different perspective. History was certainly not destined to return to "an original state": it was moving inexorably toward a future unlike anything that had gone before, when God's purpose for his creation would come to its destined fulfillment. It was a perspective that did not long prevail over the habits of mind trained in the reigning schools of philosophy; indeed, it was soon transformed into an attitude that was shared as much by Stoics as by Christians. All agreed that change was to be expected in the future. But surely this would be the change experienced by each individual at the moment of death. "Live out this day as 'twere thy last," "In the midst of life we are in death" — this was a fundamental principle of a "philosophical" as much as of Christian life. Thus living *as if* the Kingdom was imminent was soon converted into living *as if* one's own death could happen at any time — an effective spur to moral endeavor but a total abandonment of the worldview of the biblical writers.

We can chart this development in an interpretation which was imposed on words of St. Paul during the Middle Ages. Paul had written, "The creation is waiting with eager expectation. . . . it is to be freed from the shackles of mortality and is to enter upon the glorious liberty of the children of God" (Rom. 8.19-21). Within his own culture, this way of speaking of the future was perfectly at home: Paul was expressing his Christian interpretation of a future scenario that was generally accepted. But later, when all idea of a cosmic destiny had given way to the standard philosophical view that nothing in the natural order changes, and that the world is simply the arena in which each individual works out personal salvation, Paul's words, taken literally, seemed to make no sense, and desperate attempts were made to salvage an intelligible meaning. In the first sentence of the verses quoted above, we even find medieval commentators translating the word *ktisis,* not as "the creation" (its normal meaning), but as "the creature": by this means Paul could be taken to be speaking, not of the future in general, but of the future of each individual — an interpretation that does violence to the text and was certainly not what Paul meant, but which avoided challenging the understanding of time, history, and the future which prevailed at the time.

Gradually, of course, this preoccupation with death and with the fate of every individual soul began to fade, and with the Renaissance attention began to be turned again to the prospects for humanity as a whole. But these, for some hundreds of years, seemed anything but apocalyptic. The exhilaration of widening horizons of discovery in the sixteenth and seventeenth centuries, and then the sense of inexorable material progress in the nineteenth, made it seem that humanity was set on an upward path that would lead to ever greater prosperity, contentment, and power over the natural environment. Throughout this period the eschatological imagery of the Bible seemed to have lost its relevance. In English churches, the medieval murals of doom and judgment had been painted over and replaced by the royal arms; and in both scholarly and popular accounts of the life of Jesus the emphasis on an imminent future radically different from the present was played down in favor of a portrait of one who was fundamentally a teacher of timeless truths about God and humanity. But by the beginning of the twentieth century the clouds had begun to gather over this bright prospect. Warfare had always been a recurrent feature of human history, but its effects on populations had been relatively limited. Now, with the invention of increasingly destructive armaments, it was becoming a major threat to civilization; and these same weapons, available to ruthless dictators, were placing unprecedented power in the hands of men of evil intent. Concerted efforts to control the belligerence that is apparently endemic in human nature (such as the creation of the League of Nations) were proving ineffective; and, as that most violent of centuries advanced, it became ever harder to anticipate a prosperous, or even a settled, future for humankind. By the end of it, the combined threats of nuclear destruction, environmental degradation, and the inevitable large-scale migration of peoples under the pressure of more widespread drought, natural disasters, and food and water shortages had begun to make an apocalyptic scenario of the quite near future seem more relevant to our condition than the optimistic predictions of previous centuries.

The Message Today

It was surely not a coincidence that the beginning of this more violent period of history coincided with the revival of interest in the language of future change, salvation, and judgment apparently used by Jesus and his followers. Albert Schweitzer's *Quest of the Historical Jesus,* first published in

German in 1906 and in English in 1910, challenged New Testament scholars to give serious attention to the gospel evidence that Jesus believed that the present world order would come to an end within a few years, that his moral teaching was an "interim ethic" sketching the type of conduct that was appropriate to the brief time that remained before the end, and that, in this respect, Jesus must inevitably appear as a "stranger" to a culture accustomed to long-term prospects of human flourishing. Much of his analysis has had to be corrected or rejected by critics on technical grounds; but the challenge has not gone away. And if, a century ago, the threatening and sometimes apocalyptic language of parts of the gospels seemed utterly "strange" and to call into question the continuing relevance and authority of the New Testament, the impact on our minds of recent developments in world history has made us much more ready to concede that language and imagery of this kind may be a more effective and relevant depiction of the human condition than the more prosaic and optimistic scenarios of previous centuries. Indeed, we hear many saying today that, even if there are still scientific uncertainties about the pace of change in the environment, even if the last half-century has shown progress in developing international instruments of control over national aggression and acquisitiveness, even if new technologies may give us the tools with which we can mitigate the consequences of past exploitation and present injustices, nevertheless the only safe course for humanity is to live *as if* the worst scenario is about to unfold around us and to take action accordingly.

In this respect, at least, we find ourselves speaking a language close to that of the Bible. And if, along with the majority of humankind, we believe in God, and draw from that belief a conviction that our creator intended better conditions for our flourishing than we have been able to provide for ourselves, then to live in anticipation of such a future, to hasten it by our commitment to make an impact on the present by acting *as if* the promised outcome were already manifesting itself, is part — perhaps a crucial part — of what it means to accept that the Bible, for all its strangeness, its contradictions, and its difficulties of interpretation, retains authority for us today. It is still "holy."

Index of Subjects

Acts of the Apostles, 21ff.
  and Paul, 23-25
  date of, 28
  historical reliability, 22ff.
  speeches in, 29ff.
  travel narrative, 28f.
  "we" passages, 28f.
adultery, 82f.
Amos, 131
apocalypse, apocalyptic, 104f., 145
apostolic, 110ff., 125
Athens, 128ff.
Aquinas, Thomas, 80
Augustine, 80, 137
authority, 17ff., 119f.
  criteria for, 18
  of Torah, 119
  political, 17f.

Baronius, Cardinal, 9
Barth, Karl, 1
Bethesda, 49f.
Blake, William, 141
Bonhoeffer, Dietrich, 1, 8

caliphate, 10, 101

Calvin, John, 113
Cambridge Modern History, 27
canon of Scripture, 4, 96
categorical imperative, 72f.
categories, 91ff.
causation, 40f.
classics, 2
collection (for Jerusalem), 23f.
confession, manuals for, 80f.
creation, 9f., 100, 142, 143
  risk involved in, 11

Darwin, Charles, 8, 121
Dead Sea Scrolls, 4
dialectic, 120
divorce, 85
Dodd, C. H., 47, 115, 117

end of the world, 135f.
Eusebius, 137
expectancy, 131ff.
expectation
  of death, 144
  of the Kingdom, 103ff.

feeding of five thousand, 48f.

Index of New Testament References

39 Meaning of 'literary'?   61 ?
   — see also 91
          — 108
         140